STRESS
What It Is,
What It Can Do to Your Health,
How to Handle It

When it was originally published, *Stress* was one of the first books to document the effects of stress on the human body—not only the nerves, but the cardiovascular, digestive, immune, and muscular systems. This pioneering work cites what we know about dealing with stress and then shows how proper diet and exercise, plus a regimen of self-care that includes such healing techniques as hypnosis, meditation, and biofeedback, can help in minimizing the damage that stress can do. Parents are offered advice on specific strategies they can teach their children to prevent the cycle of stress and illness from taking hold.

Completely updated to reflect our changing times and research that has been conducted in the past twenty years, *Stress* is a classic on the subject.

Walter McQuade and Ann Aikman are a husband-and-wife writing team.

STRESS

What It Is
What It Can Do to Your Health
How to Handle It

Walter McQuade
and
Ann Aikman

Ⓢ
A SIGNET BOOK

A NOTE TO THE READER

The ideas, procedures, and suggestions contained in this book are not intended as a substitute for consulting with your physician. All matters regarding your health require medical supervision.

SIGNET
Published by the Penguin Group
Penguin Books USA Inc., 375 Hudson Street,
New York, New York 10014, U.S.A.
Penguin Books Ltd, 27 Wrights Lane,
London W8 5TZ, England
Penguin Books Australia Ltd, Ringwood,
Victoria, Australia
Penguin Books Canada Ltd, 10 Alcorn Avenue,
Toronto, Ontario, Canada M4V 3B2
Penguin Books (N.Z.) Ltd, 182-190 Wairau Road,
Auckland 10, New Zealand

Penguin Books Ltd, Registered Offices:
Harmondsworth, Middlesex, England

Published by Signet, an imprint of New American Library,
a division of Penguin Books USA Inc.
Previously published in a Dutton edition.

First Signet Printing, July, 1993
10 9 8 7 6 5 4 3 2 1

Contents

Foreword   ix
Acknowledgments   xiii

Part One: Stress in the Take Society   1

Part Two: What Stress Can Do to You   21

  1: The Cardiovascular System: Heart Attack,
     Hypertension, Angina, Arrhythmia, Migraine   23
  2: The Digestive System and Related Organs:
     Ulcers, Colitis, Constipation, Diarrhea   46
  3: Stress and the Immunity Screen: Infections,
     Allergies, Auto-immunity, Cancer   62
  4: The Skeletal-Muscular System: Backache,
     Tension Headache, Arthritis,
     the Accident-prone   83

Part Three: How It Happens:
              The Pathways of Stress   97

  5: How the Mind Handles Stress   99
  6: How the Body Handles Stress   106
  7: How the Mind Betrays the Body   116

Part Four: What You Can Do About It—
             Personal Solutions for the
             Stress Problem   127

  8: Altering Your Equipment: Exercise and Diet   131

9: Altering Your Response to Stress:
Psychotherapy, Drugs, Support Groups,
Meditation, Biological Feedback, Hypnosis 158
10: Stress and the Drive for Success 200

Epilogue: A Second Chance 217

Appendix: A Predictive Study of
Coronary Heart Disease 224

Further Reading 236

Index 245

STRESS

What It Is
What It Can Do to Your Health
How to Handle It

Foreword

Our publisher has asked us to write a foreword for this revised edition of *Stress*, a small book, first issued in 1974, that has been reprinted numerous times in several languages.

At that time, the word *stress* (once used chiefly as an engineering term) had already entered the medical vocabulary, designating a plague in which the mind attacks the body. The old infectious diseases—typhoid, diphtheria, and the like—had been solved, but too many people were still getting sick, many of them dying before their time.

Why? One answer clearly was the increasing subjective strain of our lives: violence in the streets, the drug problem, economic fluctuations, battles between the sexes, travesty politics, rising crime and racial confrontations, poor people getting poorer, the ominous spread of nuclear power, and particularly, desperate personal predicaments.

Now add AIDS, homelessness, and other gathering catastrophes. For an analogy to the proliferating tension of our lives, draw a graph of the national debt. Ten years ago it was 994 million dollars and was considered appalling. Since then it has quadrupled, to four trillion dollars. Similarly, stress continues to grow, eroding our health.

Yet hope is growing too. Using methods that we described in 1974, then just coming into use, many people are taking personal action against the stress that is pressing them. Relaxation and yoga groups are found throughout the land. Fifteen thousand physicians now use hypnosis in their practices, and there are 1,800 licensed practitioners of biofeedback—and the costs of both these techniques increasingly are covered by medical insurance, a clear recognition of their efficacy in treating hypertension, heart disease, migraine, muscular pathology, and other common conditions. More and more physicians, too, accept the effectiveness of these adjunctive treatments, persuaded by an avalanche of research demonstrating anew the thesis of this book that the mind that harms the body can help to heal it.

Much of current stress research concerns the human brain's effect on the immune system, the means by which the body defends itself—or, in reverse, betrays itself. Nervous tissue, it has been found, permeates the thymus, the spleen, the lymph glands, and bone marrow, all important players in immune reactions. Immunological behavior is also altered by a host of chemicals that are released by the central nervous system. Scientists are identifying more and more of these chemicals and learning that a number of them are triggered by stress.

In heart disease, Rosenman and Friedman's famous "Type A" studies have been modified by more recent research that brings into sharper focus the personality traits causing people to become coronary-prone. The driving quality is not so much competitiveness itself, but the often hostile feelings underlying it: anger, compounded by a fundamental cynicism and mistrust of others. People under middle age who measure high in this kind of hostility are four to five times likelier than more genial types to eventually develop coronary artery blockage, according to studies at Duke University.

Cardiologist Dean Ornish of San Francisco treats his heart patients with all the techniques described in this book: yoga, meditation, group support, exercise, as well as a drastic diet (no meat, chicken, or fish, and only 10 percent of calories from fat, as compared to the American Heart Association's recommended maximum of 30 percent). Some patients who stick to his regime, he reports, actually show signs of reversing their disease—and the ones with the greatest arterial blockage are the ones who improve the most.

You may not be able to mediate all the external forces that buffet your life. A little stress is acceptable, even stimulating. But when the amount steps up and you feel its claws, it is time to learn how to exercise some control over both your mental state and your physiological responses.

Meditation, hypnosis, support groups, biofeedback, and the rest help you to exert that control. You can learn to lean back mentally, watching yourself in unhurried detachment as you navigate among the many stresses of our time. Your mind will become calm, your body grateful.

The original title of this book was *Stress: What It Is, What It Can Do to Your Health, How to Fight Back*. With this edition, for obvious reasons, we are changing that last phrase of the subtitle to *How to Handle It*.

Acknowledgments

A number of medical people gave generously of their time and counsel in the research attending upon this book. Most of their names will be found on its pages. We are particularly grateful to Stewart Wolf, Hans Selye, and Meyer Friedman.

Parts of three chapters of the book appeared in different form in *Fortune* magazine. The authors are indebted to the editors of *Fortune* for their original interest in the subject, and for sponsoring investigations. Special thanks are due to Varian Ayers Knisely and also Edith Roper for their intelligent and careful research, and for their companionship along the way.

We also thank Louise Campbell, who helped us research certain materials, and Mary Elizabeth Allison.

The authors, however, are solely responsible for the interpretations and opinions expressed in this book.

PART ONE

Stress in the Take Society

The past hundred years have witnessed a drastic change in the nature of sickness—and of medical practice. A century ago the average physician was a generalist with little doubt in his mind that the patient, in all his complex humanity, was the problem to solve. Sir William Osler, a famous Canadian clinician, said, "It is much more important to know what sort of patient has a disease than what sort of disease a patient has." Claude Bernard, the most renowned of nineteenth-century French physiologists, maintained that disease is resisted by a central equilibrium within the patient. Illnesses hover constantly about us, he said, their seeds blown by the wind, but they do not take root in the *terrain* unless it is ready to receive them. By *terrain* Bernard meant the human body, a collection of cells and systems that is constantly shifting, altering, adjusting to pressures from within and without.

But even in Bernard's time, medicine was beginning to forsake these notions in its excitement over the work of the great microbiologists; the focus passed from the *terrain* to the specifics of what lurked in the wind, as researchers like Koch and Pasteur began identifying and then conquering infectious microbes, one after the other. Because of their work, the great infectious scourges of eighteenth- and nineteenth-century America—diphtheria, typhus and the like—have all disappeared from the twentieth-century list of the ten leading causes of serious illness and death. Nevertheless, the hospitals are fuller than ever, and so today the old question is being asked all over again: What does make people sick?

It is the thesis of a growing number of medical scientists—and of this exploratory book—that the basic cause of much twentieth-century disease is a shadow which has slowly darkened our lives, like the smog that has darkened our cities. This shadow is stress.

A man walks down a city street late at night. He becomes aware he is being followed by three tall teen-agers. To elude them he enters a subway station and pays his fare. But the footfalls continue to echo behind him. The subway platform is otherwise deserted. His body tightens. He walks faster, still followed, afraid to turn around. This is stress.

A young woman in a big-city ghetto, the mother of three small children, has a job as a lab technician. One day she receives notification that her day-care center is closing down for lack of funds. She can't afford a private nursery. But if she quits work to take care of the children she'll have to go on welfare. This too is stress.

A businessman drives to work and parks his car in the slot with his name lettered on it, one small evidence of his success within a firm that for twenty years has sustained the good life for himself and his family. Entering his office, he finds on his desk a memo from the executive vice president: "The chairman wants a study of the savings possible in merging your division with warehousing and relocating in Mexico." He reacts with a surge of interior chemistry. Flash go the hormones into his blood; up goes his pulse beat; but he can neither confront the threat physically nor flee. Instead he plunges into a battle fought with weapons no heavier than paper clips. Under his forced calm builds repressed rage without any adequate target— except himself.

To add specifics, if this man is one of those hard-driving,

competitive perfectionists whom many corporations prize, and if this kind of stress is chronic in his life, the experts will tell you he is a prime candidate for an early coronary attack (an even likelier candidate than American men in general, whose chances of having a heart attack before age sixty have risen to one in five). If not a coronary, it might be hypertension, ulcers, asthma, emphysema, arthritis, ulcerative colitis, migraine, backache, or even the kind of scalp itch that James V. Forrestal, Secretary of Defense under Truman, developed as he began to give way to interior pressure before committing suicide. Or perhaps a collision on the road: stressed people are more accident prone.

During prehistoric times, people survived in a dangerous world because, along with an elaborate brain, they possessed the mechanisms for instant physical response when threatened. Picture the stereotypical caveman, many thousands of years ago, resting in the sun in front of his cave after the hunt. Suddenly he feels the shadow of a predatory animal, stalking. Without thinking he reacts with a mighty rush of automatic resources. His heartbeat quickens. His blood pressure rises. Into his blood pour hormones that send sugar to his muscles and brain, mobilizing full energy. His digestive processes turn off at once so that this energy, undiverted, can be directed toward meeting the threat. Red blood cells flood into the arteries to help the body take in oxygen and cast off carbon dioxide. He clubs the intruder—or flees into his cave.

Animals respond this way still. A snake coils and strikes. A lion springs. A deer speeds into the bush. But when modern men and women feel threatened, various constraints of twentieth-century civilization compel them to clamp a lid on their instinctive impulses. Over the course of time, medical science now tells us, the accumulated effects of these frustrated physical reactions damage the circulatory system, the digestive tract, the lungs, the muscles, and the joints, and hasten the general process of aging. We don't *catch* migraine, or coronary disease, or perhaps even cancer, despite the virus theory. These sicknesses happen to us because we are rendered vulnerable by the way we choose to live—or, more often, the life that has chosen us.

Stress disease is relatively absent in some parts of the world. In Gabon, Africa, the infant mortality rate is 229 per thousand compared with 19.8 here, but coronary thrombosis at age forty is almost unheard of. And in a few sections of the globe, for example parts of the Caucasus, people live unusually long lives, sometimes well past a hundred years. What usually characterizes these communities is not the perfect diet, or clement weather, or the absence of harmful habits like smoking and drinking. Rather it is a kind of social serenity, together with simple physical work in which the young and the very old both have a contribution to make, a place in the social organization that is securely their own.

Neither does stress strike all individuals equally. Some people seem to thrive on it; it is their meat—Winston Churchill comes to mind. If you spend your life doing something that really matters to you, and doing it well, you can withstand a great deal.

Most of us do not fare so well. For airport flight dispatchers stress is endemic. Assembly-line mechanics, waiters, taxi drivers, college students competing to get into medical school—all are anything but immune. People living in a rapidly deteriorating neighborhood know stress well. All social shifts generate stress, and there are signs that women's vulnerability is increasing as fast as their independence. A century ago peptic ulcers were a woman's ailment, by a ratio of seven to three. Then, as frontier rigors were replaced by industrial ones, life got easier for women and harder for men, and from 1920 to 1940 nine out of ten victims were male. But since mid-century the incidence of ulcers in women is again on the rise.

Stress, of course, is nothing new to humanity. From time immemorial all people—and to a degree all animals—have shared three fundamental stresses, passed down over the centuries as part of the primordial heritage.

The first of the primal stresses is the threat of mortal combat. It is a threat that most Americans seldom have to deal with physically, but television and the newspapers are full of it, and it is an important influence in people's lives. It figures in dreams, and underlies anxieties.

When combat threatens, the caveman reaction occurs. The heart starts beating faster; blood pressure rises; the digestive system slows down; and numerous other changes take place, all automatic and all aimed against the enemy. These changes occur not only to troops in combat, but to children frightened by strange noises in the night, and to men and women caught up in the rarefied game of office politics. The changes are useful to the troops; but they only make a frightened child more fearful, and in the long run they can have a deadly effect on the ambitious person trying to outmaneuver competitors. These are physical changes designed to facilitate physical action. When we need to fight or run, they help us. But when we don't, they still occur—and if the emergency doesn't pass, if the threat isn't met and solved, these changes persist and become chronic, wearing out the motor of the body without taking us anywhere.

The second primal threat to survival is the basic problem of getting enough to eat—or, early in life, of being given enough to eat. This is a problem everyone faces in its original, primordial form: we all begin life as infants needing to be fed. Fighting or running is useless here, even if an infant could fight or run. What he is up against is not an enemy to be defeated, but a source to be persuaded.

When food is given, attention is given, recognition is given, love is given; and when food is withheld these other things are withheld too, so that children's feeding experiences soon become mixed with all kinds of feelings about themselves and their value in relation to other people, and also about the giving and receiving of anything between two individuals. People with dependency problems, people who feel they don't receive what they deserve in life, are likely to develop stomach problems. Wanting makes them hunger, literally.

The third primal threat to survival differs from the others in that it is a problem with no solution. You can attack or flee an enemy, you can yell for food (or love, or money) and at least have hope of results, but what can you do about the certainty that one day you will die?

To begin, you can try to make your life worth living, for as long as it lasts. You can also turn for reassurance to religion or philosophy. Even the steeliest of atheists believes in some depth of himself not that God exists, perhaps, but that he himself will survive. Conversely, the most serene believer knows in his soul what lies ahead of him, and goes in fear not only of death itself, but of those occasions when death's prospect will rise to confront him. It confronts him in particular when he gets sick.

The phenomenon of religious belief is a large subject, but viewing it just from the point of a book about physical illness, it must be said that religion in a devout believer has little equal as an allayer of stress. This is true of all religions, but particularly true of some. The Judaic-Christian tradition, for instance, takes on all the primal stresses, and if it does not dispose of them completely it makes them surprisingly bearable. Whatever role you play in your world, however humble, it argues, is an important role, created by God for a reason. It tells you that you can't win them all, and that the people who seem to win them all don't really win. Winners are often losers in the end, because winning isn't what matters anyway but meaning, truth, and love—and in the case of Christianity, life everlasting. And it tells you that God loves you and will go on taking care of you no matter what you do. Religion condemns sin, but in the very act of condemning makes a place for it. Unlike some systems of ethics, which seem cold and narrow by comparison, most religious creeds expect the individual to sin; they accept, however sorrowfully, one's need to express rage, envy, covetousness, as well as repentance afterwards—and these are all things that people need badly to express.

The waning power of religion is one reason why life has become so stressful in the Western world, and also why many people today are reconsidering, and turning once again to religious faith, the more evangelical, it seems, the more popular.

But modern societies have also lost other supports that in the past helped people endure toil, hardship and suffering: a stabilizing stoicism that most of us can no longer really comprehend; a feeling of worth derived from the exercise of individual craftsmanship—things made by hand and mind, not stamped out by a machine; a feeling of permanent place in the social order. In the twentieth century the great increase in physical abundance has been accompanied by a deep erosion of these intangible sources of strength and comfort.

Particularly potent have been the side effects of one of the industrial world's most precious products: social mobility. A black general has risen to Chief of Staff of the armed forces, and working for him are women air force pilots; women also are working as telephone linemen (and men as operators); homosexuality has come into the open. All these developments, almost unthinkable only a generation ago, proclaim our growing freedom. We value this freedom, and rightly so, but perhaps we should be more realistic about the price we pay for it. Assuming we are free to succeed, we are thereby free to fail. This is the land of opportunity, and God helps those that help themselves. Thus each individual is thrust into an endless race in which losing or lagging becomes proof of profound personal inadequacy. And in the course of this race we are constantly measuring ourselves against our competitors. When they gain, we lose.

Ours is a "take" society, so much so that while everyone knows immediately what the word "take" means—to grasp, to go out and seize possession of— defining the word "give" requires thought. Giving has to do with a pouring forth. It may take the form of love, or of philanthropy, or of teaching, or of art, or simply of a relaxed and easy adjustment to circumstance. It needs a certain abundance, but not an industrial one. Real giving does not depend on repayment; no deal is involved. Mozart did not write his forty-one symphonies for money or acclaim, though he badly needed both; he wrote them because of the music inside him.

The Mozarts of the world usually produce, regardless of obstacles; ordinary people, however, are more limited by the temper of their times. If the mark of success in life has very little to do with what you give and almost everything to do with what you take, you get a society like ours, with its emphasis on ambition and status, on cars and weedless lawns, on culture as acquisition rather than as enjoyment. A take society has a lean and hungry spirit, a spirit of meanness and jealousy. Enough is never enough. We are aware something is missing, and we are right, but the only way we know to fill the emptiness is by going after still more cars, larger lawns, taller office buildings, and more elaborately equipped cultural centers.

Industrialism itself works hard to project a philanthropic image, the image of the all-bountiful giver working round the clock to satisfy people's needs through a procession of increasingly ingenious products. Perhaps this conception is historically valid, but industry by now is not so much responding to the age-old needs of people as working to arouse new ones, whipping up longings for products that we never missed when they did not exist. The products aren't gifts anyway, obviously; we "take" them by working hard to amass the money or the credit necessary for their purchase. And we do not really need to receive more anyway. What we need to learn now is to give. But when the culture cannot teach us how, when the only way to regain the balance is through the individual, this imposes great stress on the individual.

Industrialism has changed our lives in other ways too. Because of it, we now possess machines by which we control our environment to a degree unimaginable in earlier times. The new question is: How are we to control the machines? From nuclear arms down to personal computers, this is the problem that confronts us, and it has much to do with the stress of ordinary life. Take the automobile. It will carry you across the continent in seventy-two hours. It will deliver you to work each day from a home twenty miles distant, thus making possible the American suburbs, the most luxuriant locale for middle-class living known to history. It has enlarged your life. It has liberated you. It has empowered you.

Hasn't it?

Ask yourself this question the next time you fight your way those twenty miles through the rush hour, feeling simultaneously bored and tense, trapped in a jam at the bridge, worried about your fuel supply, prey to that ominous cough from under the car's hood, and substantially in debt to the agency that helped you purchase the beast. To what extent has the automobile freed you? To what extent has it enslaved you?

The machine age is very hard, too, on the human body. The body was designed for physical use, marvelously designed—in fact it is probably the only piece of equipment in your life that improves with work. Every time you exercise your word processor or your dishwasher machine they lose a little. Every time you exercise your body, it gains.

Our bodies know this, but they don't know anything about the machine age. We keep telling them to be quiet, we don't need them any more, except maybe to push a button or shift a gear, but they won't listen; they keep clamoring to be used.

Perhaps more than anything else, the twentieth century believes in change—and change itself can stress people, as is shown in a study by Thomas J. Holmes of the University of Washington. Holmes and his helpers spent twenty years following hundreds of individuals as they wandered through the land mines of modern life: their wives or husbands suddenly died or filed for divorce; they were fired from jobs; a family fight broke out; they were forced to pull up stakes and move from one part of the country to another; their sexual lives fell out of adjustment. Or perhaps there was a sudden change for the better: a longed-for pregnancy; a promotion at the office.

Holmes rated the impact of these life changes on a scale starting with 100 for the most serious, death of a spouse, down through such events as divorce, rate 73; being sent to jail, 63; being fired, 47; and thirty-nine other occurrences, right down to going on vacation, 13; and getting a parking ticket, 11. He called the numbers Life Change Units.

Over the years Holmes weighed these Life Change Units against the health of his subjects. High scores, he established, precipitate the common stress diseases; and he warned that an accumulation of more than two hundred units in a single year is more than the average American can take without getting sick.

But sameness, too little change, also produces stress. If people are brought to a standstill, balanced motionless against threatening forces—especially forces they cannot deal with in physical ways—they will often give way and develop an organic illness as a literal expression of their frustration. Mistaken marriages often do this to people, aging them fast, settling them into the routine of least resistance. Prisons do it too.* So do offices, shops, and factories.

* But how a prison is run is often more important than length of confinement. Following World War II, Dr. Harold Wolff of Cornell University-New York Hospital made an exhaustive study of American servicemen who had been prisoners in enemy camps. He found that of the men imprisoned in Europe, fewer than one percent died before release, while the mortality rate for those in Japanese camps was one in three. The average prisoner in Asia was held much longer—forty months, as compared with ten months in the European camps. But the discrepancy in deaths was so large that Wolff began seeking other factors. He found that nutrition and medical care were roughly similar in the two kinds of camps. What was different was the degree of purely emotional stress. The Germans were by no means gentle to their military captives, but in the Japanese camps conditions were far more demoralizing, filled with terror and humiliation.

What happened when the war ended and the survivors were brought home? "Six years after liberation," reported Wolff in his book *Stress and Disease* (edited by Stewart Wolf, Charles C. Thomas, publisher, Springfield, Illinois, 1953), "the fate of those who survived the Japanese prison experience was investigated. In the first place, the total number of deaths in the group was three times as great as in the group of United States prisoners of war in Europe. Moreover, the cause of death included many diseases not directly related to confinement or starvation: twice the expected number of heart disease, more than twice the number of cancer, and more than four times the expected number of disease of the gastro-intestinal tract. Twice the number died from suicide—and most striking of all, three times the expected number died as a result of accidents. Nine times the expected died of pulmonary tuberculosis."

So do tense neighborhoods, particularly in a huge and run-down metropolis. The submerged vindictiveness of people trapped in the big cities was demonstrated by psychologist F. G. Zimbardo. He parked an automobile on a street in lower Manhattan and, as part of the same experiment, he also parked one in a much smaller city, Palo Alto, California. In each case he selected middle-class neighborhoods near universities—New York University in Manhattan and Stanford in Palo Alto. He left the hoods of the cars up to indicate mechanical trouble, and then retreated behind a nearby window to observe.

In New York City it took just seven minutes for vandalism to set in, and by the time sixty-four hours had passed, Zimbardo reported, the car was "a battered, useless hunk of metal, the result of twenty-three incidents of destructive contact." Most of the culprits worked by daylight, and were well-dressed, white, middle-class adults. By contrast the car parked in pleasant Palo Alto went unharmed, although not untouched. When rain began to fall a kindly pedestrian stopped and lowered the hood to keep the motor dry.

If people lose hope of changing their situation, anticipating just more of the miserable sameness day after day, year after year, disspirit can breed specific disease, with symptoms which conventional doctors can chart and follow, but not always understand—and very seldom cure. Humans are dynamic, meant to move forward. It is by adjusting to change that the species has evolved, and that its individual members grow and develop. This is true even of the elderly: a study at a hospital in Tuscaloosa, Alabama, indicated that one cause of senescence is the loss of challenge in the lives of aged patients.

Modern men and women, then, prey on their own physical health, and that of their family and friends; frustration and unhappiness grate together to make them sick in body as in spirit. Is there anything they can do about it?

This book offers some answers to this question. Some are quite old, derived for Western use from placid Eastern spiritual traditions. Others are as subtly European as psychotherapy, or as ebulliently technological as biological feedback. All involve management of emotions, and of challenges. Some are easy to undertake; others require a complex voyage into self. Central to them all is a return to a consideration of the wholeness we need as humans to survive medically, and the necessity to take action ourselves, not merely sit in doctors' waiting rooms.

The first wave of systematic stress research, dominating the field in the '30s, '40s and early '50s, was the psychosomatic movement, which labored to define those personality types most likely to contract ulcers, heart trouble, migraine, arthritis, and other specific ills. That work continues to stand up, yet it has not turned out to be as useful as was first hoped. Not all "coronary types" suffer coronaries, nor do all heart-attack patients possess a "coronary personality," and the correlation is even lower in such complex afflictions as arthritis and diabetes. For these reasons, and also because of recent major discoveries in biochemistry, the emphasis today has passed to the physical and chemical pathways that stress takes within the body. But both approaches are fruitful, and between them they set the stage for an assault on disease no less radical than Pasteur's laboratory work or Sigmund Freud's definitive cataloguing of neuroses and psychoses.

In the middle of this century the man who stepped forward to occupy the stage most prominently was Hans Selye, a slightly-built, Austrian-born endocrinologist with compelling continental manners and a brilliant and assertive mind.

I once interviewed Selye in one of his research laboratories at the University of Montreal, set in the foot-hills looking down over the city. His book-lined office was snug. Selye sat in a high-backed leather swivel chair with one foot tucked under him. His shirt was tie-less, the soft collar askew above his starched laboratory jacket. At his elbow was an intercom, which frequently interrupted. The voices of his colleagues scratched through in any of five different languages—this was an international center—and Selye responded in kind. He wore heavy, horn-rimmed glasses, but they were off and on constantly as he spoke animatedly, eyes gleaming, anticipating questions, skillfully shaping the conversation to get somewhere. Even diversions had a point. I learned he had a plastic hip joint, that he was very conscious of being in his mid-sixties, very impatient to move further forward in search of solutions for stress. "Life science isn't a coldly intellectual thing like mathematics," he said. "Experience counts. I am at least ten times more effective than I was at twenty-five. But I have lost so much because of deterioration."

An intimation of Selye's life work came to him in his early manhood. He recalled, "I was a second-year medical student in Prague when my professor brought in five patients for the students to diagnose—one with cancer, one with gastric ulcer, et cetera. It struck me that the professor never spoke about what was common to them all, only about the differences. All these patients had lost weight, lost energy, and lost their appetites. Had I already been a physician at that time, I wouldn't have thought about it, but as it was I asked my professor if I could work on it in my free time, but he thought it was silly.

"That was in 1926. Ten years later, as assistant professor at McGill in Montreal, I was trying to isolate a hormone in the laboratory. I was working with extracts of cow ovaries and injecting them into rats. All of the rats, when later subjected to stress, had the same reaction—adrenal overreaction, duodenal and gastric ulcers, and shrinking thymus, spleen and lymph nodes. The worse the stress the stronger the reaction. Then I tried injecting other materials, even simple dirt. I even tried electric shock, and got the same results.''

He also tried inducing fear and rage in the laboratory animals. Again he got the same physical results. From this puzzling beginning, in which he discovered the existence of a generalized reaction to almost any kind of stress, he gradually groped toward the conviction that the endocrine glands, particularly the adrenals, were the body's prime reactors to stress. He said, ''They are the only organs that do not shrink under stress; they thrive and enlarge. If you remove them, and subject an animal to stress, it can't live. But if you remove them and then inject extract of cattle adrenals, stress resistance will vary in direct proportion to the amount of the injection, and can even be put back to normal.''

Selye defined stress as the nonspecific response of the body to any demand made on it. He explained that when the brain signals the attack of a stressor—which could equally be a predatory beast, or a threatening office memorandum—the pituitary and adrenal glands produce such hormones as ACTH, cortisone and cortisol, which stimulate protective bodily reactions. If the stress is a fresh wound, the blood rushes inflammatory substances in to seal it off; if the stress is a broken bone, swelling occurs around the break. The pro-inflammatory hormones are balanced by anti-inflammatory hormones, which prevent the body from reacting so strongly that the reaction causes more harm than the injury.

The initial response to any kind of stress is alarm. It is followed by the stage of resistance, a chemical rallying of the body's defenses. The fight is on—even if the body, in effect, is just fighting the mind. If the threat is prolonged, an exhaustion of resources sets in, as the defense system gradually wears down. Selye called this process the General Adaptation Syndrome. His most significant breakthrough came when he discovered that he could take two similar groups of rats and predispose one group to heart disease, an affliction rare in any kind of lower animal, by injecting an excess of sodium and certain kinds of hormones. None of the control group suffered. All the rats in the predisposed group died shortly of heart disease.

Stress is not only a killer, Selye emphasized, but also a drastic wearing force. Different people have different hereditary capacities to withstand stress, he held, but once each person's "adaptation energy" has been expended, there is no known way to replenish it. Selye believed that some time in the future it may be possible to produce from the tissues of young animals a substance that could restore human adaptation energy. "But that is for the Jules Verne future—soft research, like soft news, that may or may not happen."

Selye likened each person's supply of adaptation energy to a nation's deposits of oil; once the man or woman has summoned it up and burned it, it is gone— and so, soon, are they. If a person blunders into a distressing marriage, or embarks on a consuming, competitive career, he or she spends that portion of adaptation energy fast and ages fast. Coffee and Dexedrine don't add to the reserve—they just let you use it up faster.

Long acknowledged as a top endocrinologist and biochemist, Dr. Selye also ventured out of his specialized territory into the larger subject of how people should live their lives. This diversion bothered some medical men, but it made Selye himself a particularly interesting scientist. His recommendation, put simply, was to work very hard in life at something that interests you and that you are good at. The aim of life, he said, is self-expression—an aim usually difficult to fulfill in our industrial society.

It is because of Selye's insights and long devotion to the chemistry of stress that many of the narrowest of physicians have come to agree that stress is indeed a genuine disease of our time. Even Louis Pasteur himself finally reached that conclusion more than half a century ago. Lying on his death bed in 1895, he reflected once again on his long scientific disagreement with Claude Bernard. Pasteur's dying words were: "Bernard was right. The microbe is nothing, the *terrain* is everything."

PART TWO

What Stress
Can Do to You

CHAPTER 1

The Cardiovascular System:
Heart Attack, Hypertension, Angina, Arrhythmia, Migraine

When you feel threatened, even by such a minor sensation as stage fright, it is your cardiovascular system which most clearly responds, changing the entire tempo of your body. The pulses pound. Blood pressure rises. The hands turn cold as blood is diverted from the skin to the vital organs.

If this temporary adjustment becomes habitual, a number of conditions may develop, ranging from simple arrhythmia—a chronically eccentric heartbeat—through hypertension, to the dreaded coronary attack.

The heart attack is a very modern affliction. Most of mankind's major illnesses have been described in medical literature as far back as Hippocrates' day, but coronaries are not among them. Even as late as the 1920s the disease was still relatively uncommon in the United States. The late Dr. Paul Dudley White recalled that in the first two years after he set up practice in 1921 he saw only three or four coronary cases. The growth in coronary heart disease seems to follow in an almost eerie way the rise in gross national product: it is as if the advanced industrial nations had some kind of patent on this ejection device of the jet age.

Some years ago, Ancel Keyes of Minnesota and other nutrition experts virtually convinced this nation that a diet high in cholesterol (featuring large quantities of meat, eggs, butter and other saturated fats) was responsible for the epidemic of heart trouble. Their evidence included a particularly plausible study of the incidence of heart trouble among those Japanese who remain in Japan, eating a very low fat diet, compared with those who emigrated to Hawaii, who ate a diet somewhat higher in saturated fat, and those who moved on to the U.S. mainland, who generally shared the American diet, high in hard fats. In this study there was virtually no heart trouble among the Japanese subjects in Japan. In Hawaii, there was some. In the U.S. the emigrants' heart trouble was on the usual elevated American scale.

Some subsequent research cast doubt, however, or at least confusion, on the Keyes study. The Harvard School of Nutrition did an exhaustive investigation into the health of 579 men who migrated from Ireland to Boston, men with brothers who remained in Ireland, where the consumption of saturated fat, especially butter, is among the highest in the world. Although the emigrants to America actually ate less saturated fat and thus were presumably safer, they had more heart trouble than their kin in Ireland. Finnish farmers eat a high hard fat diet and have a lot of heart attacks. Masai tribesmen in Africa take in an even higher fat diet, and have none.

The mystery remains: Is it really the consumption of hard fat by mouth that raises the level of cholesterol and other dangerous artery-clogging substances in the blood? Not exclusively, it would seem, for even in the U.S. many people who consume such diets have low cholesterol ratings. Dr. Ray Rosenman, a San Francisco cardiologist, and a member of one of the leading heart research teams in this country, says, "Diet, exercise, family history, and blood cholesterol are important, but the thing that has increased over the years when heart disease has grown so alarmingly is pace. Man is the only animal that perceives time, and our civilization is marked by a continually faster and faster speed. Look at England a hundred years ago. They ate the same as we do and exercised less; they weighed more than we do, but they didn't have as much heart disease.''

For hundreds of years, old wives and other medical amateurs have suspected that heart trouble is brought on by too much personal push. Some doctors have agreed. Sir William Osler lived too early to see many coronary cases, but he left a shrewd description of the angina type. "It is not the delicate, neurotic person who is prone to angina,'' he wrote, "but the robust, the vigorous in mind and body, the keen and ambitious man, the indicator of whose engine is always at 'full speed ahead' . . . the well-set man of from forty-five to fifty-five years of age, with military bearing, iron gray hair, and florid complexion.'' In short, the hero of the industrial society: the manager, the foreman, the executive secretary, the stress-driven competitor.

In the past sixty years there has been sufficient research into the correlation between physical and personality types to produce a compelling picture of the kinds of people prone to heart disease. The research is not so much consecutive as cumulative. Examining it is like peeling an onion. The outer layers are new and pungent, but as one peels back into the work of the 1930s, the evidence is in many ways even stronger. This earlier work concerns not only coronaries, but a spectrum of other cardiovascular ailments, and it tries to discover not only what kind of people are likely to get sick, but what makes them that way.

Some of the most interesting peels have been produced by Dr. Rosenman and his partner, Dr. Meyer Friedman.

Back in the 1950s these two cardiologists were deep in the study of the standard heart risk factors: cigarette smoking, blood pressure, diet, obesity, and in particular serum cholesterol. Like most cardiologists then—and now—their principal emphasis was on the build-up of fatty acids in the blood, which can eventually harden in the artery walls, narrowing the channel and keeping blood from the heart itself. Friedman says now, "I was cholesterol-oriented because I am a laboratory man and cholesterol does produce disease in animals. It was also something we could work on. So we thought, 'Let's get cholesterol down.' "

Nevertheless, puzzling factors kept cropping up—among them the low incidence of heart disease in American women. Friedman points out, "Although American women seemed to be protected from heart trouble, Mexican women were having as much heart disease as their men. It is also one to one in Southern Italy, but it is four to one in Northern Italy. An American Negress in Chicago or North Carolina has more heart disease than her husband. Therefore it can't be sexual hormones. As a good scientist—my definition of a good scientist is one who looks at the exception—I should have connected. But I didn't think it through."

One day in the early 1950s an upholsterer came in to redo the Friedman-Rosenman waiting room, and was puzzled by the condition of the chairs. The only place the chairs were worn, he said, was at the front edge of the seats. This Dr. Friedman interprets today as an indication that "Our individual patients were signaling us. Over 90 percent were showing signs of struggle in their lives."

From these simple beginnings came a program that was to involve thousands of staff hours and hundreds of thousands of research dollars during the succeeding two decades. The result was an impressive case for the idea that stress and behavior are principal culprits in the high incidence of heart attacks among middle-age Americans; that personality patterns are of vital importance; and—perhaps—that these personality patterns can be changed before it is too late.

Friedman and Rosenman took the first small step in their new direction by going to a women's club, the local Junior League, and asking its members to keep diaries of what they ate, and also of what their husbands ate. No major dietary differences were found between the husbands and the wives. When Friedman reported this to the president of the Junior League she said she was not surprised. She already knew why men got heart attacks, she told him—trouble at the office.

Next Friedman and Rosenman sent questionnaires to a group of advertising men and engineers in San Francisco, asking them what factors seemed to have preceded heart attacks among friends and colleagues, and giving ten choices of answer, including all the standard risks such as diet and cigarette consumption, plus anxiety, work, excessive competition, and stress of making deadlines. Fewer than 3 percent mentioned the normal risk items, and fewer than 4 percent selected anxiety or work. More than 70 percent picked excessive competition and stress of making deadlines.

Then came a study with accountants which involved more than opinion, and which began to attract considerable attention. Accountants were chosen for the study because their work rises and falls in intensity, alternating spells of easy routine with periods such as tax time when they knock themselves out to meet the deadline. All were asked to keep detailed diaries of what they ate, and Friedman and Rosenman arranged to examine each twice a month, measuring cholesterol levels during both slack periods and times of heavy pressure.

Two significant cholesterol peaks occurred: first, when the accountants were closing out the yearly books of their clients in January, and again in March to mid-April when they were heavily involved in preparing income tax returns. Not everyone reacted to the stress in the same degree, but there was an overall jump of fatty acids in the blood during these periods, with a falling off in months of more placid work. The correlation between work loads and cholesterol readings was direct, and was independent of individual variations in diet, weight, or amount of exercise.

At the same time they were studying the accountants, Friedman and Rosenman also began considering the matter of individual differences in temperament that might influence people's reactions to stress. No two individuals handle stress identically, but which one ends up with heart disease and which one doesn't?

"Thus emerged our Type A and Type B," says Rosenman.

Type A, either male or female, is characterized by intense drive, aggressiveness, ambition, competitiveness, pressure for getting things done, and the habit of pitting oneself against the clock. These people may give an impression of iron control, or wear a mask of easy geniality, but the strain glints through.

By contrast, Type B's are more easygoing. They are open. They are not always glancing at their watches. They are not so preoccupied with achievement, are less competitive, and even speak in a more modulated style.

Most people are mixtures of Type A and Type B, of course, and Rosenman and Friedman sharpened their interviewing techniques to the point where they could recognize four distinct subdivisions of each group, ranging from A-1, the most virulent, down to B-4, the mildest.* They also trained a number of interviewers to spot one pattern or another as dominant and come up with a convincing consensus. The standard list of questions in the twenty-minute interview is reprinted in the Appendix, page 224. As important as the questions, however, is the way the answer is spoken, in the judgment of the experienced interviewer. An impatient subject, who shows his impatience, is probably an A, no matter what he says. Some questions, as noted in the Appendix, even call for a pretense of

---

* Dr. Friedman and Dr. Rosenman go into them in detail in their book, *Type A: Behavior and Your Heart*, New York: Alfred A. Knopf, 1974.

stammering on the part of the interviewer. An A intrudes into the stammer, while B waits quietly.

The general picture that emerges of the two types is familiar, recognizable—and a bit broad. The prototypical Type A is a man who, while waiting to see the dentist, is on the telephone making business calls. He speaks in staccato, and has a tendency to end his sentences in a rush. He frequently sighs faintly between words (Dr. Friedman identifies this as "deadly—a sign of emotional exhaustion"). Type A is seldom out of his office or shop sick. He rarely goes to a doctor, and almost never to a psychiatrist—he does not feel he needs either. Indeed many Type A's die of otherwise recoverable coronaries simply because they wait too long to call for help. When necessity does force an A into a physician's hands, he is an impatient patient. One malady which is rather unlikely to strike him is peptic ulcer.

Type A is often a little hard to get along with. His chuckle is rather grim. He does not drive people who work under him as hard as he drives himself, but he has little time to waste with them. He wants respect, not affection. Yet in some ways he can be said to be more sensitive than the milder Type B. He hates to fire anyone and will go to great lengths to avoid it. Sometimes the only way he can resolve such a situation is by mounting a general office crisis. If he himself has ever been fired it is not for underachievement but probably because of a personality clash with a colleague or superior.

Type A, surprisingly, goes to bed earlier than Type B. He doesn't get much out of home life anyway, and might as well prepare for the day ahead with a good night's rest, whereas Type B will get interested in something and sit up late, or simply socialize. Type A smokes cigarettes, never a pipe. Headwaiters learn not to keep him waiting for a reservation; if they do, they lose him. They like him because he doesn't linger over his meals, and doesn't complain about the cooking. He salts the meal before he tastes it, and has never sent a bottle of wine back to the cellar.

Type A's have little time for exercise. When they do play golf it is fast through, and in tennis they can be difficult partners. On vacation they like to go to lively, competitive places and if possible to combine the vacation with business. They never return to work a day or two late; they are more likely to be back early. Most days they stay on at the office well into the evening, and when they do leave, their desk tops are clear.

But in the competition for the top jobs in their companies, says Dr. Friedman, A's often lose out to B's. They lose because they are *too* competitive—narrowly, compulsively so. They make decisions too fast—in minutes, instead of days—and so may make serious business mistakes. They are intoxicated by numerical competition: how many units sold in Phoenix, how many miles traveled in February. Life to an A-1 is a race against a clock and an adding machine. He lives by numbers in a constant effort to build up higher totals.

And even in business, higher totals aren't always what wins. In Friedman's words, "A's are dead creatively. They will add A and B and get C, where a creative B person would come up with a brilliant R." He adds, "A's have no respect for B's, but the smart B uses an A. The great salesmen are A's. The corporation presidents are usually B's."

Often you can tell an A by the way he uses his body. His hands are slightly clenched. He may have a habit of tuneless humming, or, while sitting, of jiggling a leg. He may smile a lot, but there is a grimace in his smile.

Women span the types too, Rosenman says. In one study specifically of women, suburban matrons turned out to be mostly B's, but top-level executive secretaries tended to be A's, with higher cholesterol ratings even though their diets were lower in fat. In another study, Friedman and Rosenman tested two orders of nuns. One was a teaching order, whose members were required to have Ph.D.'s. They were highly competitive, mostly Type A. The other order was more contemplative and, true to type, were mostly B's.

What is most tragic of all in this picture of hopeful, driving energy is that the Type A's are two or three times more likely than the Type B's to get coronary heart disease in middle age. In all of Sinclair Lewis's pitiless characterizations of American businessmen there is nothing so devastating as these doctors' cool statistics.

Rosenman and Friedman's pioneering study involved a total of 3,500 male subjects, aged thirty-one to fifty-nine, with no known history of heart disease at the time they entered the program. Each of these men was classified on the A-1 to B-4 scale by trained interviewers ("All the interviewers were Type A's," says Friedman. "It takes an A to catch an A.") They were also given complete physical examinations, and these were repeated at regular intervals as the program gradually accumulated data.

As of 1970, 257 of these men had developed coronary heart disease, 70 percent of them Type A's. But even more emphatic was the picture that emerged when the A's and B's in the program were compared with respect to the more conventional risk factors for heart trouble. A's got more heart attacks than B's even if they didn't smoke, even if their blood pressure was normal, even if their family background showed no coronary disease. Conversely, B's could have adverse ratings in these factors and still be relatively safe. Of the standard risks, only one seemed really important: cholesterol levels in the blood. As a group, A's had higher cholesterol than B's. And B's exceeded A's in their heart attack rate in only one situation: when their cholesterol level was conspicuously higher—more than 260 in B's, compared with 220 or less in A's. But once again: what made the cholesterol go up?

The medical debate that arose out of the Friedman-Rosenman studies was a bitter one. As notable a cardiologist as Paul Dudley White insisted that stress never hurt a healthy heart, and a number of others complained that the methods for classifying individuals were subjective, relying chiefly on the interviewer's personal impressions. Rosenman and Friedman did not deny this, but pointed out that a good deal of all medical analysis is also subjective, and that their staff of interviewers agreed with one another at least as often as a group of cardiologists going over the same cardiogram tape. Said Rosenman, "Most epidemiologists are incapable of thinking of anything that cannot be quantified. There are no positive links between diet or exercise and heart disease either. A migraine is subjective, too."

What Type A's need but cannot easily achieve is restraint, says Dr. Friedman, and he speaks out of personal experience. He is himself a high Type A, and suffered a heart attack in 1967. Dr. Rosenman, both experts agree, is a natural B.

Friedman, since his heart attack, has been carefully impersonating a Type B, even to dressing in a deliberately casual way—relaxed tweed sports jacket complete with a pipe in the pocket. "My cholesterol was 292 at the time of the attack," he says. "Afterward, in the hospital, I reread Marcel Proust's *Remembrance of Things Past,* and it fell to 210. Then I went home, still scrupulously on the same diet, and it started back up again."

His own prescription for moderating his Type A propensities: "I have changed my life style. I live in Sausalito now. We no longer go to cocktail parties, and I'm off all my committees except one. I daydream.

I go into St. Mary's Cathedral at lunch time and look at the stained glass windows." In 1972 he went to Texas for the heart-bypass operation, and gave up even his pipe.

Of the typical coronary patient he says, "He has become no longer human. You must give him back his personality. You have to pull his attention to the joys of *being*, as compared with those of *having* things which signal his success, get him away from that awful obsession with numbers.

"You have to realize," continues the doctor, "that for thirty-odd years these people have been drilling themselves to speed up. We have to de-drill them. Get them to slow down at a yellow light instead of speeding up. If they don't they should drive around the block and try again. If they are commuters, I tell them to get up earlier and dilly-dally for a while before they catch their trains.

"You can't change personality, but you can engineer a new regimen. Have him walk in parks and notice the sequence of what blossoms when. Any noncompetitive, nonmechanized kind of exercise." Friedman abhors jogging, which he calls the best way to achieve sudden death at thirty-five. "You should only start jogging if you have had a cardiogram while on a treadmill with a fibrillator right there. An A who is jogging tends to say, 'I did two miles in twenty minutes yesterday. I'll try for nineteen minutes today.' "

He tells his patients who must travel long distances never to take east-west flights on the same day they have to do business, but to allow three days because of the time difference. The advice is to arrive in the distant city the night before business in time for a relaxed dinner, work the next day, and return home the third. One is permitted to take lunch with business associates on the second day, but not dinner. "At night keep away from business. Wander about the city aimlessly."

Friedman recalls the practice of a famous Type B captain of industry, now retired, in making decisions. If the matter did not have five-year importance, he would send it to a subordinate to decide. If it did have five-year importance, he would ask himself if he could delay decision, and then would bring in some subordinates to study it. If the decision could not wait, he would go ahead and decide, but he found that this kind of problem came up only about once a month.

More than fifty years ago, at a time when Friedman was still in medical school, Dr. Flanders Dunbar and several of her colleagues at New York's Columbia Presbyterian Medical Center began mulling over the common emotional characteristics of patients with certain diseases, including hypertension, heart trouble of all kinds, rheumatic fever and diabetes. Over the course of five years, they studied some 1,600 of these patients—not a specially selected group, just the normal hospital population. Each was given a psychiatric examination, and relevant facts such as age, upbringing and family sickness were also checked. The results, when finally correlated, were startling. Four out of five patients were discovered to have character traits and emotional problems peculiar to their disease group.

Dr. Dunbar's research into heart attacks does not dispute any of Friedman and Rosenman's later findings, but she did dig deeper into the personality they have since labeled Type A, and she also investigated the traits of the victims of other common cardiovascular ailments: hypertension, angina and cardiac arrhythmia.

In Dr. Dunbar's heart attack patients, men outnumbered women six to one, and she, like most other physicians, labeled their affliction "a middle-age male disease." She observed that the coronary-prone have great difficulty sharing responsibility and find it hard to get along with their superiors. Many of them are self-made men or highly trained professionals. Their overriding personality trait she described as "compulsive striving. They would rather die than fail. The more difficult things become and the more unhappy they become, the harder they work. . . ."* Physically they take poor care of themselves—they eat the wrong kind of food, and try to replenish their energy with coffee and cigarettes. Socially they are "successful" but without much enjoyment of it all. Their style of conversation is highly rational and often a little argumentative, and they cannot express their inner feelings easily. They tend to keep people at a slight distance.

When this kind of person is struck down by a heart attack his first response, Dr. Dunbar observed, is usually a basic despair which sometimes turns into extreme depression. More often than not, however, he pulls himself together again, says that nothing is seriously wrong, and against his doctor's orders resumes his driven existence as soon as he can possibly manage it. Whereupon he very often dies of a second attack.

Why is the coronary patient this way? Dr. Dunbar's study reveals a number of common patterns in the background. One of these patterns is heart disease in other people the patient has known, especially in his mother—although the fact that the person involved was often not a blood relative suggests that nongenetic factors may be important. Another background item: as children and young adults, both men and women of the coronary group tended to identify with their fathers, although at the same time they also felt a good deal of hostility toward them. They were fond of their mothers, whom they found easy to dominate; but their fathers they were determined to outdo by rising to a

* Flanders Dunbar, *Psychosomatic Diagnosis*, Paul B. Hoeber, Inc., 1943.

high position in life. Many of them succeeded in this, and then, as adults, showed a marked tendency to cut both parents out of their lives.

The father became translated in adult life into the boss, whom they surpassed if they could, or tried to get the best of if they couldn't. They were easily hurt by their superiors. When this happened they did not walk off the job, but curried favor and tensely bided their time, in anticipation of another contest of wills.

Dr. Dunbar identified the biggest off-job problem in these patients as family and sex. Most of the women in the group were frigid and most of the men had frigid wives. She attributed this situation to the intense drive of these patients, to their difficulty in accepting partners of any kind, and also to the grind of the long hours they kept, the lack of vacations, and so forth. But the coronary patient was found to be repressed in many other ways too, held in by unconscious curbs on all his instinctive drives. Conflict, even with his superiors at work, was pushed out of his conscious mind, to seethe and roil just below the surface. And he succeeded in keeping it there by means of his great defense: work.*

"Coronary patients," the Dunbar study reported, ". . . are strong only in the sense that the highly unified and rigidly crystalized life role is culturally well adapted and very rewarding." But then something goes wrong. Events jar the job, a decision made in haste turns into a disaster, the rewards fade just as the current goal is in sight. And all that deliberate self confidence begins to crack. It is then that heart attacks strike.

Dr. Dunbar was working in the 1930s, a decade so

---

* In fact, as Dr. Stewart Wolf has observed, the coronary type, despite his long hours, usually fails to find real satisfaction in his work. He should not be confused with another kind of striver—the person who pushes himself hard because his career is especially fulfilling, and who is no more coronary prone than the general population.

strenuous that the mortality from coronaries increased more than 100 percent in the United States during just four years. Self-destruction was in the air, and the self-destructive heart attack became almost a way out for those who were overwhelmed by this particular brand of stress. Mere advice did not help her patients. She decided to try psychiatry.

She found that psychiatry could be quite effective with the coronary patient, despite his habitual distrust of doctors. "The coronary patient is a particularly satisfying person with whom to work therapeutically," she wrote. "His lifelong habit of working things out for himself makes it easy to enlist his interest and co-operation . . . in none of the cases . . . were the results anything but favorable." She warned other practitioners, however, about the same enduring independence in the coronary-prone, about the "frequent cheerfulness of these patients, their tendency to joke and take it like a good fellow. This is not an indication of a good adjustment to the illness, as is so often assumed, but simply one more expression of the patient's characteristic, and in terms of emotional economy, damaging behavior pattern. In our series the patients who were the 'best sports' about their illness were the ones who died."

HYPERTENSION

In hypertension, the heart pumps blood to the body under abnormally high pressure. The causes, it is agreed widely, include emotional stress. More women than men suffer from hypertension.

The prevalence of hypertension rises and falls from one country to another, reflecting various cultural tensions. It is a frequent cause of death in Japan, for example, though almost unknown in other areas of the Pacific. In the United States it is a common disease of blacks in the large Northern cities; it seldom occurs among the black population of Africa.

Blood pressure fluctuates in healthy people as well as in sick people, sometimes rising because of the actions of the heart muscle, sometimes because the arteries resist the normal flow of blood. Dr. Harold Wolff of New York Hospital found that these two different mechanisms for elevating the blood pressure have their psychological parallels. He called the first type the "exercise pattern." It can be produced by physical exertion, such as running, or by emotional disturbance. The heartbeat goes up in an effort to push more blood through the body, without necessarily encountering more resistance. Dr. Wolff found that when he interviewed people of this type they seemed to be quite willing to express their feelings and conflicts.

The disease known as essential hypertension, however, is caused by arterial constriction, which actually reduces the flow of blood through the body. This is what occurs normally when a healthy human suffers a cut or hemorrhage: the arteries contract and the blood thickens in an automatic effort to minimize loss of the essential fluid. The person suffering from essential hypertension maintains an exterior calm during interviews, but a professional can discern evidence of strong underlying feelings. In a sense she, or he, is unable to bleed emotionally.

Hypertension is of course dangerous, and can lead to heart attacks, strokes and kidney damage. The single question that patients on the examining table most frequently ask their doctors is still: "How is my blood pressure?"

Wolff illustrated the effects of stress on blood pressure with an example from history: the battle of Stalingrad in World War II, when Russian soldiers resisted, block by block, the stubborn German effort to conquer their city, in three long years of disorganized carnage. This was a pitting of individual against individual, an ordeal of isolated personal peril. The result was a virtual epidemic. During 1942 and 1943, the hypertension rate rose from 4.1 percent of the population to 64 percent. And these people did not return to normal after the siege lifted; most of them were dead by the early 1960s, well before their time.*

Flanders Dunbar's study found both similarities and some definite differences between heart attack patients and patients with high blood pressure. Typical hypertensives are just as ambitious in their way as the coronary type, she reported, but a great deal less self-confident. They, too, spend their lives in unspoken conflict with authority, but they have little expectation of winning that conflict, with the result that they may imprison themselves early in a job beneath their capacities, with little responsibility and little future.

Often in childhood they had bad relationships with their fathers and were not allowed to talk back, so that a mixture of anger and guilt has built up inside them, to be directed in adulthood against their employers, or in the case of some husbands and wives, against each other. Hypertensives' relations with their mothers were close, and remain so—they never really succeed in breaking away as the coronary type does, and throughout their lives swing back and forth between a longing to be taken care of and resentment against overprotection. Hypertensives are easily upset—by criticism, by disorder, by imperfection of any kind—but do not know how to handle upsetting situations. They are by turns anxious to please and longing to rebel. They will explode in irritability one day, then the next subside into a kind of limp willingness to put up with anything

---

* War stresses people in ways that are not always predictable, however, and the results can be surprising. When English cities came under savage air attack in World War II, the incidence of ulcers increased but two other prime indices of stress, alcoholism and suicide, declined markedly. Personal problems have a way of fading, apparently, when a community must rally to fight off disaster.

for the sake of peace—and neither approach solves their problems. Nor do their customary forms of solace: liquor, sex, food and cigarettes. In fact these often help to bring on the illness, which usually follows some precipitating event—perhaps separation from a loved one, or money difficulties—by a period of several months, during which the person eats, drinks, and smokes too much and gets involved in love affairs, breaking through his—or her—normal reserve into what Dr. Dunbar described as "volcanic eruptions of irritability, humor or sentiment."

In the case of most female patients, the trouble almost all hypertensives have with authority becomes especially important in their relations with men. One of Dr. Dunbar's cases, an unmarried woman of thirty-six, was a classic example. In childhood, though she was fond of her mother she hated her father. Both parents were strict, and she received almost no sexual education. Partly as a result she became pregnant at sixteen (her illegitimate baby later died), and then went on to contract syphilis, at which point, embittered, she gave up sex altogether. There ensued a long career of low-paying menial jobs under employers she could not get along with, and gathering illness in the form of high blood pressure, finally culminating in a fatal heart attack while she was still in her thirties.

Quite apart from her sexual experiences, this patient had no wish to marry. Before her death she told Dr. Dunbar, "All men do is boss you around, they don't take care of you anyway, so I'd rather take care of myself and be my own boss."

Hypertensives turn out to be quite responsive to psychiatric counseling. Their many conflicting needs—for dependence versus independence, for failure versus success, for self-indulgence versus self-punishment—constitute a good handle for a competent therapist.

In counseling, a therapist will sometimes leave the blood pressure cuff strapped around the patient's arm and from time to time take a reading in order to ascertain the effect on the patient of certain sensitive subjects.

Dr. Dunbar did this in the case of a twenty-two-year-old man who had three times been rejected for service in the Navy during World War II because of hypertension. Son of a naval officer, a husky six feet two inches tall, seldom ill, he was reported by his worried father to have scored a blood pressure of 150/90 when applying for Annapolis, and then on three attempts for the Navy itself, from 180/130 to 180/140. His father could see no signs of emotional trouble, or even mildly errant behavior. "He never drinks, smokes, or gets mixed up with girls."

The young man's mother had died some three years earlier—from high blood pressure—and when Dr. Dunbar asked if the boy had been upset the father answered, "You wouldn't believe it. That big, strapping youngster went all to pieces. He was like a baby."

Then the son came in for a session. Dr. Dunbar found him seemingly undisturbed, except for the matter of his rejection by the Navy. His blood pressure registered a high 180/130, however, and the cuff was left on his arm. After twenty minutes of rather random discussion, she pointed out to him that the pressure had gone down to a normal 135/90. "We then discussed his mother and her death. He stated it was probably a good idea she had died, that he had never really liked her as much as he liked his father, and that since he had known for about six months that she would probably die he had not been in the least disturbed by it. While he was talking, I took his blood pressure again and called his attention to the fact that the reading was 185/130. This startled him and opened the way for discussing his real feelings about his mother, his ambivalence toward her, and his conflict with his father. When he left his blood pressure was again 135/90.''

After another session with Dr. Dunbar, he took his Navy physical and passed it with a blood pressure reading of 138/90.

ANGINA AND ARRHYTHMIA

One way of reacting to stress is ordinary neurotic behavior, and there is reason to believe that people who have developed this pattern are better off in terms of physical health than people who haven't. Two forms of heart disease—angina, and cardiac arrhythmia—are cases in point.

Angina is the illness in which not enough oxygen reaches the heart: the symptoms are stabbing chest pains and a feeling of suffocation. The disease is less serious than a heart attack, and the people who get it are often paler versions of the coronary-prone. Success is important to them, and so is money, but they do not feel the desperate drive to outdo everyone in sight, the insatiable craving to beat the boss, that runs the coronary personality ragged. But above all, though both are inwardly neurotic, angina patients show it more. They are aware of underlying fears and anxieties, and they express them in their behavior, in the form of nervous tension, moments of impulsiveness, and sometimes various phobias. They dream more, and are apt to have an active fantasy life.

If people with angina are rather neurotic in behavior, most people who suffer from arrhythmia are more so. An attack of arrhythmia is a direct demonstration that the heart is malfunctioning. It is very frightening, and once it happens, it can set off a panicky pattern of recurrence. Yet there is no organic damage that can be discovered. In fact, the condition is often called cardiac neurosis.

Arrhythmia patients, Dr. Dunbar found, are moody, fearful, and full of conflicting feelings. They frequently swing back and forth between gaiety and self-disgust; between powerful longings to "win" and a fear of rousing hostility; between an easy pleasure in friends and a mistrust of them. Many have dreams of smothering, and they long to escape the problems and conflicts of their lives. One told Dr. Dunbar, "It may sound funny to you, but it used to be a relief to have a real pain to fight, instead of my husband and all the people I hated."

Despite these distinctions, however, patients with different forms of heart disease tend to resemble one another in basic personality and behavior. Their traits overlap, just as their diseases do, and of course patients who have had heart attacks often go on to develop angina or arrhythmia.

MIGRAINE

Headache seldom kills, but that counsel is of little comfort to anyone suffering from the merciless throbbing it can mount in the skull. Thomas Jefferson, a migraine victim, said, "The art of life is the avoiding of pain."

Headaches cause more than half the visits to doctors' offices in this country, as well as a sizable proportion of TV commercials for over-the-counter medications. Of the disabling and periodic types, migraine strikes one in eight Americans at some point in their lives, and is caused by dilation of the blood vessels in the scalp. It thus qualifies as a cardiovascular ailment. A distinctly different kind of headache, the kind due to muscular tension, is discussed in Part Two, Chapter Four, but migraine's pain is so devastating that it can bring on tension headaches too, pain attracting more pain.

Characteristically migraine attacks only one side of the head at a time, and it is often very regular in its visits—perhaps hitting on the same day, same hour, every week. More women than men get migraines, but the very worst pattern of migraines—clusters, which occur in close series—claim more men than women. Before the migraine settles in, its victims frequently experience what is called aura: the arteries in the scalp first constrict, causing strange visual effects, or the feeling of nausea. Then the arteries react by dilating, and the painful interior pounding begins.

Several decades ago Harold G. Wolff made a pioneering study of the relations between migraine and personality, and today his work is still considered definitive by the experts. In connecting stress directly with migraine, he pointed out a paradoxical twist. It is not during the periods when stress is bearing down hardest that migraine patients usually get their headaches. Instead, it is when the pressure lifts and they are, so to speak, off duty. It often comes on leisurely weekends. Sunday is a notorious migraine day.

Perhaps the truth is that many migraine patients don't know what to do with leisure; for them, as for the coronary type, the meaning of life is work. But coronary types work hard in order to dominate their world, while migraine patients have rather different motives.

At bottom most of them are insecure, according to the Wolff study. What they really want is to be loved, but they will settle for being admired, or simply approved of: anything to still the gnawing sense of worthlessness. It is for this reason that they drive themselves so hard, selflessly taking on thankless chores, burdening themselves with ever-increasing responsibilities, conscientious, rigid, somewhat fanatical.

It isn't surprising, then, that when leisure finally does catch up with them they crack. It is then that migraine strikes—and with it, often, many long-buried feelings. In fact the patient's whole behavior may change, if only for the duration of the attack.

Treatment of migraine in this country has been mainly by drugs: aspirin, of course, to raise the pain threshold, and ergotomine tartrate (frequently mixed with caffeine) which constricts the painfully dilated arteries. Before the modern era of medicine, magic was commonly used, often effectively, and even today placebo pills help a surprising number of patients. One migraine sufferer, a butcher by trade, has discovered he can cure his attacks simply by spending ten or fifteen minutes inside his walk-in freezer.

But the best results occur when the physician helps the patient understand not only the physical workings of the arteries, but the ways in which emotions may be affecting them. In Part Four, Chapter Nine, is described a very new and promising treatment for migraine that involves the will and the mind, with no drugs at all.

CHAPTER 2

The Digestive System and Related Organs: Ulcers, Colitis, Constipation, Diarrhea

While the heart is a constant presence in the body, setting its whole tempo with that steady beat, beat, beat, the stomach is quiet for hours at a time. But it too knows how to assert itself when the moment comes. It furnishes the body a yearning: hunger. We not only need to eat, we want to, from the moment the infant squalls its demand for mother's milk, up through the years of childhood and their blazing hungers, to the only slightly less passionate, if more discriminating, fascination that adults feel for food.

The fact that eating forms so much of our social apparatus, that the act of savoring, for example, is such an integral part of partying, that courting means having dinner together, that breakfast and supper remain the central rituals of family life—to say nothing of the infamous business lunch—closely connects the taking in of nourishment to all the subtle complications of our private lives. It isn't surprising, then, that when you are under pressure, the body's clearest signal of that fact may come when you swallow. The effects turn up in the esophagus, the stomach, the duodenum, the small intestine, the colon, including the sigmoid and rectum, and all the links and locks in between. Other organs involved in the processing of food, such as the kidneys and pancreas, are also frequent victims of stress.

* * *

The digestive system begins at the mouth, where food is chewed and salivated and then sent down through the esophagus to the stomach. The stomach takes the food and continues the breaking-down process—kneading it with vigorous muscular contractions and attacking it with hydrochloric acid and enzymes, aided by the hordes of bacteria which abound in the lower intestinal system. The small intestine and, to some degree, the stomach select the substances that the body can use and pass them into the blood stream. What remains is then sent on to the colon, a flexible tube about three inches in diameter and over four feet long. The colon does absorb further water and salts, and some vitamins are manufactured in it by bacterial action, but its main function might be called transportation. Its contractions propel waste into the rectum for final disposal through the anus. By the time feces are ejected, a relatively small percentage is actual food residue, except for cellulose. Most of it is material shed by the walls of the digestive system, bacteria, gas and water.

The digestive system treats food as the mind treats life itself, accepting most of it, mulling on it, savoring its flavors, extracting what it can use, and outright rejecting some of it. Like the mind, the digestive system is affected by nuances and seasonings—many of which the mind provides. The metaphoric capacities of the human gastro-intestinal tract are well known, and their links to the emotional memories of early childhood are obvious both in the matter of eating, and in the first of those many educational courses humans must master to get along in their world, toilet training.

Before going further into the gastro-intestinal diseases and their personality prototypes, it is worth pointing out what a tremendously hardy apparatus the human digestive system is when nothing is worrying it. It has been demonstrated that any irritant tolerated by the skin of the forearm can also be tolerated within the healthy stomach. In fact the lining of the stomach is tougher than the exterior skin: stomach acid, when mixed with pepsin (one of the stomach's two protein-digesting enzymes) can actually burn a hole in the skin of the arm.

It was Dr. Stewart Wolf who made the most definitive study of the effects of emotional stress on digestive function; in the process he enlisted a layman whose situation in life made him an invaluable associate—a man identified in medical literature simply as Tom.

Tom's father worked in the railroad yards in New York City, and on a very hot day in the summer of 1895, he brought home what looked like a "growler" of beer from the corner saloon. The pail, however, actually contained scalding hot clam chowder left over from a political rally the night before. While his father wasn't looking nine-year-old Tom made the mistake of gulping a large mouthful of the stuff, and was afraid to spit it out on his mother's clean floor. His esophagus was so severely seared that the burned surfaces became welded together, despite emergency medical treatment, and were sealed off in scar. To get food into Tom's stomach, surgeons at a hospital made an opening through the abdominal wall, which, for the next sixty-five years, was the only entry he could use. For a period after his injury he had to be fed by his mother, the food an unsavory gruel poured into the opening. Between meals the opening was bandaged.

His medical problems aside, Tom had, by today's measure, a hard life; the child of working class parents of Irish extraction, he left school at the age of ten to help support his family. But one of his strongest drives, perhaps partly because of his bizarre eating method, was always toward conventional respectability. In time he learned he could consume almost any dish and enjoy its taste by first chewing it in his mouth, then transferring it to his stomach for the rest of the digestive process, but the procedure embarrassed him and drove him into seclusion at feeding time, except with a few people he particularly trusted. Wolf wrote: "His diet differed little from what it might have been had he been able to swallow. Seated next to a table, with his feet propped up on a chair, he chewed his food and spat it into a funnel inserted into the fistula. He took a great deal of liquid with meals in order to wash the food through the narrow neck of the funnel, and particularly liked beer. After tasting the first few sips he often simply poured in the rest in order to save time."*

After starting his working life as a plumber's helper Tom wandered hopefully for almost forty years through a succession of other jobs in the mechanical trades, always concealing his peculiarity from the world. He particularly shunned medical men, and for thirty years did not reveal his stomach condition to any doctor, until finally in the depression of the 1930s, working as a shovel man with a WPA crew, he hit a stretch of digging that irritated the stomach opening, made it bleed constantly, and finally brought him, weak and wan, to a hospital for help. Two years later he met and was befriended by Dr. Wolf, at that time a young medical resident studying at New York Hospital under the renowned Dr. Harold L. Wolff, who has already been quoted more than once in this book. Both the middle-age doctor and the young one were keen students of the effects of the emotions on a wide range of organic disorders, and in Tom they found a subject with difficulties in life and dramatic visceral patterns for expressing them. They got him a hospital job, as orderly and messenger, and initiated a series of observations and tests that lasted over a period of years. There have been other "gastric fistula" patients in medical history, but none were studied so thoroughly as Tom.

* Stewart Wolf, *The Stomach,* Oxford University Press, 1965.

What the medical world learned by way of Tom has filled several books, but to summarize the most important conclusions, Wolf established beyond contradiction that the mucous membrane lining which protects the inside of a person's stomach is clearly affected not only day to day but minute to minute by both conscious and unconscious emotions. When Tom was angered, either by life itself, or by aggressive "stress" interviews, the lining of his stomach became as inflamed as the skin of his ruddy face; his stomach also over-functioned, producing an excessive amount of acid, and the mucous membrane was assaulted by the strong gastric juices, even producing a clearly visible ulcer at one point. In contrast, when life seemed hard and the future looked very pale to him, the lining of his stomach turned pale too. His stomach underfunctioned. Insufficient acid was secreted, a condition which produced varying degrees of nausea.

The best cure was emotional—either an improvement in Tom's life, or the friendly assurance by Dr. Wolf that things were not so bad, really. Another form of reassurance, placebos—bogus pills—also helped at times.

Tom spent more than fifteen years under study at New York Hospital, although Stewart Wolf left to join the Army Medical Corps in World War II and was away for several years. In 1952 Wolf moved to the Southwest, to head the department of medicine at the University of Oklahoma, but he continued to see Tom at intervals, looking after him—and into him.

In 1956 Tom developed a cancer in his stomach which was successfully removed, but in the process the opening in his stomach was enlarged. This made it hard for his body to retain fluids, and during the next two years the stress of the situation gave rise to ulcers. Tom did not know what to do. He wanted to consult Stewart Wolf, so Wolf brought him to Oklahoma for treatment and persuaded him that further surgery was necessary. In the end, though, Tom changed his mind and refused to undergo another operation. He returned to New York and died soon after, at the age of seventy-three. Wolf wrote: "Thus ends the story of Tom—faithful friend and collaborator—in whose stomach we were able to study an experimentally induced peptic ulcer and later a carcinoma with atrophic gastritis. Finally, in a setting of controversy with his old friend the experimenter, he developed peptic ulcers. None of these lesions were responsible for his death. He died because we were not skillful enough to persuade him to undergo a surgical revision of his stoma."

ULCERS

When infants do not get enough affection and reassurance while being fed, it may demoralize them, or at least their digestive functions, permanently. Unconsciously, in later life they connect feeding and love and long deeply for both. Some may develop a weight problem, from constantly nibbling on snacks whether hungry or not. Some may become compulsive eaters, prey to secret, panicky binges in which they gobble up everything in sight till they vomit. Others may turn into one of the estimated eight million Americans, male and female, who suffer from ulcers.

People with stomach ulcers have gastric systems that are in constant motion, or, it could be said, in constant emotion. They are always hungry. Their digestive juices run full time whether their bodies actually need nourishment or not. Even the most conservative of internists will admit that there is an "ulcer type" whose tendencies are inflamed by conventional life stresses, a highly competitive man or woman, a go-getter—often a business executive, of either sex—who drives for independence from the rest of the world and for conventional success in life, while holding down the even stronger unconscious urge to be nurtured and taken care of. These people are usually found to be full of hostility, but they are blocked off from expressing it—they want too much to be loved. The right kind of marriage is particularly important to them. If one finds a mate of considerable tenderness, able to comfort and sustain, the ulcer type can still compete in business hours and not sustain stomach pains. But many, of course, do not find the right mate.* Doctors Edward Weiss and O. Spurgeon English wrote in their standard work *Psychosomatic Medicine* (W. B. Saunders Co., Philadelphia, 1943): "Bed and board in adult life are as indissolubly connected as sustenance and sensibility in infant life. . . . Men with functional disturbances of the stomach have a very high incidence of marital difficulties." This was written many years ago; today it is more true of the distaff side of marriages as well.

Here is an ulcer case as described in Stewart Wolf's *The Stomach:*

> A forty-four-year-old civil service employee had complained of gnawing epigastric pain on and off for twenty years. His father had been a gentle, retiring person, and his mother a matriarchal woman intensely ambitious for her children. His two older brothers were able to adjust satisfactorily to this setting, the oldest by graduating from medical school and the second one by adopting a rebellious attitude and becom-

The Journal of Chronic Diseases in 1961 published a study by Drs. Sidney Cobb, Stanislav V. Kasl, John R. P. French and Guttorm Norstebo titled "Why Do Wives with Rheumatoid Arthritis Have Husbands with Peptic Ulcers?" The authors answered that the wife in such a marriage, conditioned by her childhood and upbringing, has a yearning for high public esteem, an ambition her husband will not help her to gratify. The husband is the common ulcer type, in strong need of emotional support which the wife, because of her resentment, does not provide. So the wife's bones and the husband's digestive tract ache to a common beat.

ing a professional gambler instead of a lawyer as his mother had wished. The patient felt the need to compensate for his brother's indifference and took premedical work at college, but he did poorly. He switched to engineering and after further failure abandoned college. In this setting he had his first symptoms of ulcer pain, and a duodenal ulcer was demonstrated by X-ray examination. He later obtained a civil service job as a draftsman, and became engaged to a warm, sympathetic girl. Symptoms disappeared during this interval, until the girl died of rheumatic heart disease a few months later. The patient's mother also died at approximately the same time. Within a few months he married an authoritarian, cold and financially ambitious woman. She disapproved of his social relationship with men friends and eventually forced him to give up lodge activities from which he had derived great satisfaction. Shortly after his marriage, the patient's ulcer symptoms recurred, and they have remained chronic ever since. Several exacerbations and two episodes of hemorrhage have coincided with periods in which his wife seriously disparaged his competence as a man. An experiment illustrated the relevance of his conflicts concerning his wife to his gastric disturbance.

Experimental study

Ten minutes after the end of a spontaneous period of vigorous gastric motor activity and during a period of almost complete absence of (stomach) contractions, an interview was undertaken in which the patient was reminded that in contrast with the high regard in which he had been held by his lodge associates, his wife considered him inadequate as a provider, companion, and sexual partner. He became grim, tense, and clenched his jaws frequently and said, "It's been a fight all along, and now I got no more fight left in me. I'm caught like a rat in a trap." Promptly, powerful gastric contractions began, and by the end of the interview, a state of sustained contraction of his stomach wall had been established. Acid secretion was greatly increased, exceeding even the level observed during the earlier period of spontaneously increased gastric function. By this time the subject had begun to groan with pain. Shortly, as strong efforts at reassurance and diversion were begun, the evidence of gastric overfunction subsided and with them the symptoms.

In treating ulcers, doctors most commonly resort to drugs, more rarely to surgery. In the operation called gastrectomy, portions of the stomach wall are cut away, not only to remove the ulcerated sections but to decrease the stomach surface and thus eliminate some of its acid-secreting capacity. A more significant surgical solution, endorsing the fact that ulcers can be caused by emotions, is the procedure of severing the vagus nerve, the transmitting line by which the brain sends its messages to the stomach. Vagotomy does usually lower the output of acid, although there are occasional side effects, ranging from diarrhea and nausea to loss of weight.

But the purely surgical approach is often unsatisfactory in the end. Gastrectomy patients, if they neglect their daily Zantac, very commonly develop ulcers again after a year or two. Even cutting the vagus nerve, though it may do away with the ulcer, doesn't always solve the real problem. A patient who has come to depend on gastric symptoms to achieve a precarious emotional balance may react to the operation by looking for other psychosomatic ailments, or by lapsing into a mental depression.

The opposite of ulcers, a slowdown of stomach function, as mentioned in the case of Tom, can be caused by general discouragement or depression. Too little acid and pepsin are produced. In this way people exposed to sudden danger lose all appetite, and sometimes become nauseous, or vomit. An infectious disease can do the same thing, especially when accompanied by fever. In cancer of the stomach, interestingly, even when the cancer starts as an ulcer lesion, the affliction seems usually to slow down the secretion of stomach acid, and there is surprisingly little pain. The predominant emotion is dejection rather than the inner rage of ulcers.

THE BOWELS

Some people are wryly proud of their ulcers as battle citations in the war of life. But there are equally disturbing ailments lower in the alimentary canal which make for little social discussion past the cruder years of childhood. These are the troubles of the irritable colon, prone to constipation, diarrhea, or, as is not uncommon, an alternation of both annoyances, and are commonly traced back to unreasonable toilet training in infancy. The extreme of this problem is ulcerative colitis, when the wall of the colon becomes so damaged that bowel movements are bloody and uncontrollable. This is a stress-related ailment which not infrequently results in early death.

The connection between bowel disorders and toilet training has been established through countless psychiatric case studies. Franz Alexander offers as an example the child who is rewarded for a bowel movement by being given a piece of candy. "In some such manner," he writes, "the excrement becomes associated with the concept of possession. This explains its close relationship to money, which is one of the best-established facts uncovered by psychoanalysis. Every excremental act is evaluated by the child as a kind of donation to the adults, an attitude often reinforced by the mother's great interest in the child's excrement."*

Sweeping—even bizarre—as this judgment may seem, most of us can provide corroboration for it from life. The emotional overtones of the two most common afflictions of the bowels have been widely noted. Con-

*Franz Alexander, *Psychosomatic Medicine*. W. W. Norton and Co., Inc., 1950.

stipation is associated with depression and dullness, diarrhea with panic. Both are centered in the colon, which, like the stomach, is designed to work intermittently, not continuously. When it overworks the result is diarrhea; when it underworks, constipation; and stress is often the culprit in both. In physical appearance the constipated colon is distended, relatively flaccid, and pale in color. There is little contractile motion. The colon of someone suffering diarrhea is narrow, taut, short and inflamed in color, swept by frequent contractions.

Constipated people are often going through a period of dejection. They are discouraged, bored, and rather grim—determined to keep on going, but with little ambition to do much more than that. Those suffering from chronic diarrhea own more flaming feelings: anger, resentment, hostility, sometimes vague guilt, a terrible touchiness toward being slighted by people or events. On the surface, however, they customarily wear a manner of polite passivity.

Hundreds of pills and potions are available from the pharmacy for both conditions, of course, and some of them work, at least temporarily. But when the patient comes under great stress—either on life's surface or in his subconscious—the medicines are of brief effectiveness. Real relief from constipation is best bought by a turning upward of the current of life itself, some good breaks. The cloud of depression drifts off, or is somehow driven off. Relief from chronic diarrhea can result from a lessening of the tensions of life that panic the colon; for example, when you begin getting along better with the in-laws with whom you share a house, or when you move away from them. When someone gets rid of an onerous financial obligation and starts living within his means, he may get rid of diarrhea too.

The bowels sometimes become a major preoccupation which can itself build up immense misery in a patient. Doctors Weiss and English quote Dr. P. W. Brown of the Mayo Clinic in a description of how this happens:

A patient of either sex, but usually a woman between the ages of twenty-five and forty-five years, comes in with the chief complaint of stomach and bowel trouble. During the narrative her memory is frequently refreshed by reference to her notes.

Her abdominal troubles date back five to twenty or more years, and consist chiefly of distress from gas, bloating, soreness in the right lower abdominal quadrant, and constipation, with occasional attacks of diarrhea which follow catharsis. The stools often contain considerable mucus, and if they are hard, bloody streaks are noticed. The distress has been present more or less all these years, and bears no regular relationship to meals or types of food. The woman never has been strong, although able to attend to usual duties and social demands. Moderate exertion, such as that accompanying a morning of shopping, or having a few guests for dinner is followed by much abdominal distress and fatigue. Dull headaches and a nagging backache are added burdens.

Further, the woman gives the history that because of the distress referable to the abdomen and back, she submitted to an operation, in the hope that appendectomy and straightening of the uterus might help. Prior to the operation, a roentgenologic examination had suggested the presence of chronic appendicitis. Relief was obtained for about three months when the same or even more marked symptoms recurred. Opinions were expressed that perhaps the gall bladder or adhesions might explain the symptoms. In view of the occasional bloody streaks in the stool and anal discomfort, treatment of hemorrhoids was carried out with relief of these local symptoms. Some time later the question of possible focal infection was raised and tonsillectomy was performed. As symptoms persisted, further investigation resulted in a diagnosis of "chronic colitis." In consequence a succession of diets was recommended: no fried or greasy foods, no starches, no meats except fish and breast of chicken, proteins and carbohydrates not to be taken at the same meal, only raw fruits and vegetables, only cooked fruits and vegetables, and so on. These diets have resulted in a distaste for food, fear of everything to eat, loss of weight, and actually more or less a state of deficiency. As a logical accompaniment of diet the arch demon, colonic irrigation, was invoked, and the irrigations soon made the mucus and distress worse, in spite of thorough flushing. Other roentgenologic studies resulted in a report of falling of the colon and stomach, for which an abdominal support was prescribed. Almost incidentally, reference is made to peculiar or difficult environmental, social and economic problems, but these are the basis of much, if not all, of the physiologic disturbances . . . the patient eagerly asks, and all in one breath, "Is the gall bladder diseased and will its removal cure colitis? Will continual abdominal irritation make a cancer? What can be done to restore the normal position of the fallen organs? Just what should my diet be? Are my adhesions causing my trouble? . . ."

Physical examination reveals an apprehensive, undernourished woman. The abdominal wall is relaxed and all muscles are flabby. A large tonsillar tag is present on the left side. Tenderness is present on palpation of the cecal region. Bimanual examination of the pelvis discloses only retroversion of the uterus.

The laboratory data are as follows: Roentgenologic examination of the stomach gives evidence of an apparently normal organ. A cholecystogram indicates that the gall bladder is functioning normally. The mucosa of the rectum is normal. No roentgenologic evidence of organic disease of the colon is elicited. The roentgenograms depict the expected influence of the abdominal support on the position of the colon.

The present condition of this hypothetical case is obvious; it is the end result of *doctoring the bowels*. Interpreted as a group, the diagnosis in such cases is that of functional intestinal disturbance associated with a state of physical and nervous exhaustion. Usually there is a greater or lesser degree of biologic inferiority, for which the patient is hardly to blame. It is this, with the characteristic emotional, nervous instability, that makes for so much difficulty.*

ULCERATIVE COLITIS

In ulcerative colitis, the membrane of the colon so deteriorates that it bleeds a great deal, and may eventually perforate. Many factors may be involved in this malady, including the immunological system (see following chapter). But whatever may be the exact coincidence of events, the personality profile of the usual victim bears a recurrent set of characteristics, say leading specialists, and the patients' sufferings are made even more miserable by the intensification of stress in their lives, whether it is easily identified pressure from job or family, or long repressed neurosis planted in childhood.

A deep feeling of utter helplessness is common among ulcerative colitis patients. This is easily understandable, once the demeaning affliction has begun within a person's bowels. Specialists in the field argue, however, that feelings of helplessness frequently precede the onslaught of the illness, and that the patient's prior emotional state helps render his or her colon vulnerable.

These patients are usually very tidy, restrained people, frequently a little prim, notably mild and mannerly, conscientious, punctual, and inhibited in the normal patterns of their lives. They are also unusually thin-skinned, alert to real or imagined insults from the world. They fear rejection and so make but few advances toward other people. Ingratiating and seemingly submissive, they have few firm friends.

What they do have is very strong, special attach-

*Edward Weiss and O. Spurgeon English, *Psychosomatic Medicine*. W. B. Saunders Co., Philadelphia, 1943.

ments, usually toward older people, whom they often end up marrying. Male patients in particular tend to marry wives who are really mother substitutes. Such marriages are frequently unhappy, partly because of sexual inhibition. Few men or women with ulcerative colitis seem to have enjoyed active, satisfying sex lives.

So close is the attachment toward one or two people that the ulcerative colitis type sometimes feels within himself that he is a proxy, or even an appendage, of the other person's personality. Often this dominant figure is a woman, and, of course, the emotional path leads back to the patient's mother, who, as described by the patients themselves, is frequently cold, or masochistic. She enjoys being a martyr, particularly to a sick child.

The bondage with such mothers is never broken. When the inevitable pressures of the world descend on the ulcerative colitis type, when he or she feels abandoned, left alone, unprepared to deliver some deed the world is demanding, the resulting despair is expressed through the gastro-intestinal equipment.

In their book *The Human Colon* Doctors William J. Grace, Stewart Wolf and Harold G. Wolff analyzed nineteen random patients, fifteen women and four men who had been plagued with ulcerative colitis for periods of six months to twenty-four years. Psychiatric interviews and counseling over the course of many months exposed many characteristics:

> . . . The women were fastidious housekeepers. One woman had a weekly housework schedule which she followed almost to the hour. Another insisted that each piece of daily used chinaware be in its own fixed place, with the handles of the cups all pointing in one direction. If this order were disturbed she became uneasy and as soon as possible restored the objects to their "proper" place. Daily scrubbing of the bathroom and kitchen floor and all the woodwork was part of another patient's routine. One patient found so much

housework to do in a three-room apartment that it occupied her whole day. One patient washed and sterilized each object or toy her two-year-old child threw out of its playpen before giving it back to the child.

Overdependence was usually observed in attitudes toward mother, parent-substitute, or spouse. Exacerbations of colitis usually occurred when their dependent position was threatened by unsympathetic behavior or by separation from or illness in a loved one. . . . One patient accompanied her husband, a salesman, on every trip he made, even if it were only for a day. Another woman felt happy and secure and relatively free of symptoms only on weekends when her husband came home. A male patient had an exacerbation of his illness during his wife's menopause when she was irritable and unable to provide him with the show of affection to which he had become accustomed. One woman lived for twenty years of her married life in her mother's home because she felt she could not get along without her emotional support.

This overdependent attitude was reflected by most of the patients in their need to please other people and to be on good terms even with casual acquaintances such as shoe clerks and delivery men. One woman said, "I can't stand anybody being mad at me." In all of the twelve married patients sexual adjustment was poor.*

The principal treatment of the nineteen patients was counseling, in addition to conventional medical care. Each was seen every few days or weeks, depending on need, the total time per patient ranging from twelve hours to twenty-five or more. Success was reported with eleven patients, slight improvement with two. No success at all was reported in those patients who would not, or could not, accept the physician as a friend, eager to help with solving the pressures of daily life.

*W. J. Grace, Stewart Wolf, and Harold G. Wolff, *The Human Colon*, Paul B. Hoeber, 1951.

CHAPTER 3

Stress and the Immunity Screen: Infections, Allergies, Auto-immunity, Cancer

It is Saturday afternoon, and Elise and David Fischer are expecting friends for dinner. David is shelling shrimps and Elise is rolling out piecrust when the phone rings.

It is Leon Harris. "Dave, I'm sorry but we've got to cancel. Franny's mother's in the hospital. The biopsy was positive; she's scheduled for surgery Monday morning."

"Leon, hey, too bad."

"Yeah. Listen, I better run—we're catching the five o'clock plane."

David hangs up and passes the news to Elise. They commiserate. Then they confer about the evening ahead. They hardly know the Spragues yet; do they really want them all by themselves? Maybe Molly and Everitt could fill in. Elise picks up the phone.

No luck. Everitt's arthritis is acting up. He's in bed with a bottle of Advil.

Suddenly the doorbell rings, and their problem is solved. It is Anne Sprague, clutching a box of Kleenex. "I thought I was better yesterday," she croaks, "but now I'm running a fever again. I guess it's the flu. I'm really sorry."

So the dinner party is off. In silence David peels a final shrimp, while Elise contemplates the unfinished pie. Then they step out onto their balcony. It is a fine spring afternoon. The grass glistens in the sunlight. The maple trees are flowering.

Suddenly Elise sneezes. The roof of her mouth begins to itch, and her eyes to water. Her head starts filling up. Her hay fever! Swiftly she steps inside again, pushing the door shut behind her, and hastens to the medicine cabinet, thinking, "What's happening to everybody?"

Two common threads run through the disparate afflictions that cancelled the Fischer's dinner party. One of these threads is the immunological system. This is the system designed to protect the body against infection. But it doesn't always work fast enough—hence, Anne Sprague's flu. And sometimes it makes mistakes. One of its commonest mistakes goes by the name of allergy—Elise Fischer's problem. And most medical authorities now suspect that a faulty immune response is also a prime factor in cancer, and that it may help to cause arthritis.

The second thread is stress. Run-down people get infections more easily, and stress runs people down. It isn't only a matter of insufficient sleep, or too many cigarettes. It is now known that stress actually disturbs the immunological system itself. In the words of Hans Selye, "If a microbe is in or around us all the time and yet causes no disease until we are exposed to stress, what is the 'cause' of our illness, the microbe or the stress?"

The science of immunology has a curious history. For centuries, infectious disease was mankind's biggest single health problem. One reason our ancestors had fewer heart attacks, of course, is that many of them didn't live long enough—diphtheria, smallpox and cholera carried them off first. But with the discoveries of Pasteur and Koch, all that began to change. Slowly but surely vaccines and antitoxins began appearing against most of the age-old microbial killers. For a hundred years the immunologist was the hero of medicine.

Then in the 1940s, penicillin appeared, presently followed by the antibiotics, and all at once immunology began to look like a dying enterprise. Why spend years developing a vaccine against a disease when you can snuff it out in a day or two with pills?

Paradoxically, it was only at this time that the study of immunology began to come into its own. Because its practical applications seemed to be fading, the work in the field began to broaden and deepen, and the result has been a surge of new research, some of it conflicting, much of it as yet inconclusive, but fascinatingly full of implications about some of the most esoteric aspects of human physiology. As a field of investigation immunology today holds a position like that of nuclear physics in the thirties; it is a place where things are happening, where major breakthroughs impend. Meanwhile, of course, antibiotics have not turned out to be all that was hoped. They're useful, but no substitute for immunity, and so the search for new vaccines flourishes once more.

When these new breakthroughs come, few doubt that they will clarify the role that stress plays in the complex workings of the body's immunological system, as described in the next pages.

INFECTIONS

When a person is in good health it sometimes seems that the human body is a fortress against infection, with a capable crew of tireless guards—known in immunology as antibodies—on patrol night and day, keeping the interior clear of the enemy. But it is not that way at all. Actually, we are tenanted with microbial agents just as thickly, and as essentially, as feudal lords were surrounded by serfs—with many of the vassals living in the castle twenty-four hours a day, covertly eying the silver goblets, tapestries and swords. When the lord's control begins to slip, the vassals may suddenly turn on him and take over.

Nevertheless, the lord could not get along without his serfs; nor can we do without the microbial life that teems within us. It assists in the digestion of food, for example. And we can tolerate even its injurious members, so long as we keep strong. Some of them we control by limiting their numbers. Others remain harmless because they are restricted to certain parts of the castle. Germs that can cause encephalitis if they enter the brain are commonly present in the healthy throat. The skin is not bothered by staphylococcus albus, but let it enter the abdominal cavity, as sometimes happens in surgery, and you may be in trouble. In fact the more sealed-off the organ, the more susceptible it is to infectious agents. The unbroken skin can withstand almost any insult. The central nervous system, the heart valves and the joints are all highly vulnerable.

The best points of entry for a microbe are the orifices of the body, especially the mouth and nose, because these are gateways for the intake of air and food, and inevitably a swarm of microbes comes along too. But usually the body knows how to protect itself. The lungs, when they exhale, expel foreign bodies that entered on the inhale—explosively at times, with coughs and sneezes. Saliva in the mouth contains chemicals deadly to many microbes, and those that survive pass down to the stomach where hydrochloric acid continues the slaughter. The wax in your ears is another protective device, as are the tears that form in your eyes.

Even when the skin is broken—when, so to speak, the wall of the castle has been scaled, and foreign invaders climb in—the body is still well designed for defense. It seals off the enemy near the point of entry, by the process known as inflammation. The skirmishing exacts a price. An inflamed area of flesh hurts, and there is some destruction of tissue; if the inflammation is severe it may impede normal functions for a while. But when it works—as it usually does—it is worth it. The invaders are cut off and surrounded, and then white blood cells come in to destroy them. In a few hours or days the job is done, and healing repairs the damage.

Some attacking microbes, eager for command of the castle, are tougher than others—so tough that inflammation alone cannot handle them. When this happens the body falls back on its last, and strongest, line of defense: the complicated mechanism known as specific immunity.

Specific immunity is the ability of the body to distinguish between self and not-self, and having made the distinction, to destroy the not-self elements. What is startling about this ability—indeed, somewhat fantastic—is that it resides not in some advanced organ like the brain, but in a part of the body one is hardly aware of—the lymphatic system. The lymphatic system contains cells known as lymphocytes, and each of these lymphocytes carries on its surface a certain kind of molecule called an immunoglobulin molecule. The brain wouldn't recognize a foreign microbe if it saw one, but these minute immunoglobulin molecules can and do.

Just how they do so was a subject of controversy for many years, but today the so-called clonal theory is generally accepted. According to this theory, each of the immunoglobulin molecules in the body has its own special shape and electrical charge, designed to fit the shape and electrical charge of a specific foreign protein molecule in the world outside, much as a key fits a lock. The first time one of these foreign molecules penetrates the defenses of the body, it sooner or later meets up with its matching immunoglobulin molecule, which then proceeds to attach itself to the invader. The invader is called an antigen. And the immunoglobulin molecule which attacks it is known as an antibody.

When antibody attacks antigen, a number of events occur. First, antigens reside on the surface of the invading microbe, and are used by it to gather food, so when they become smothered by antibodies the microbe begins to starve. This smothering also prevents the microbe from releasing chemical substances that can damage tissues and destroy white blood cells.

But something more drastic also happens. The lymphocyte that houses the antibody, known as a T-lymphocyte, begins to reproduce, creating more and more T-lymphocytes, each containing the same antibody specific to this particular antigen; and a second type of lymphocyte, the so-called B-lymphocyte, is in some way stimulated to change into a plasma cell.

A plasma cell is basically a manufacturing plant. What it produces is the same antibody that the T-lymphocytes produce, only in far greater numbers. And these antibodies produced by the plasma cell do not remain with the parent cell as the antibodies of T-lymphocytes do. They are released into the blood and circulate to almost every tissue of the body.

If this is the person's first encounter with the microbe in question, a week or two—sometimes longer— will pass before these so-called humoral antibodies—the ones manufactured by the plasma cells—become numerous enough to handle a major invasion. During this period, the patient is sick. Inflammation makes him hurt in assorted places. He feels tired and weak because so much of his energy goes into building up his defenses. He may even run a fever. But fever helps too, because it speeds antibody production, and in some cases it may affect the invader more directly. A microbe that flourishes in a 98.6-degree environment may start to wilt at 103 degrees.

Even after the patient recovers, his plasma cells continue for months to manufacture antibodies against the now defeated antigen, so that should it return it can be dealt with promptly. If no second invasion occurs, however, antibody production gradually drops, until by the end of a couple of years a test of the patient's blood will show that he is approximately back where he started.

And yet he is *not* back where he started—that is the marvel of specific immunity. If the same microbe finally launches another attack, in some fashion the person's defending lymphocytes will recognize the old enemy and go to work a great deal faster—so fast that in most cases the person won't have time to get sick. Inflammation and fever aren't necessary. The instant proliferation of antibodies overwhelms the invasion before it can get under way.

Which is why measles and mumps are one-time diseases.

Then what about flu and strep infections, not to mention colds—the nuisance diseases, that recur over and over in the lives of perfectly healthy people?

The answer is that none of these is a single disease. There are some fifty known varieties of strep bacteria in Group A alone. The common cold is nothing but a set of symptoms which can be set off by any of approximately a hundred microbes. And over the years these microbial agents have a way of mutating—that is, of altering the genetic structure passed on from parent microbe to child microbe, which alters the antigens, which in turn means you lose your hard-won immunity. In other words, although theoretically you could acquire immunity to all hundred forms of the common cold, through several years of constant coughing and nose-running, by the end of that time the first forms on your list would have mutated and you would have to start over again.

The body's defenses against invasion do not operate full force at all times. In the first months of life the immunity screen is still under construction, and in old age it begins to deteriorate: both babies and the elderly are very susceptible to infection.

And so are people under stress. It is well known that stress weakens the immune response, by specific physical pathways that are being widely studied. One of the things that happens is that emotional problems rouse the hypothalamus in the brain.* The hypothalamus then rouses the pituitary gland. The pituitary rouses the adrenal glands. And the adrenals start sending out increased amounts of a kind of hormone called a glucocorticoid.

These excess glucocorticoids can do a lot of damage, for under their influence people produce fewer antibodies, and their inflammatory response dwindles. Experiments have shown that when polio virus is injected into the brains of hamsters, 27 percent will die of the disease, but if accompanied by a strong shot of cortisone the death rate rises to 100 percent. In real life the results may be less dramatic. Nevertheless, when problems are piled on problems and the last thing you need is to get sick, it is precisely then—and precisely because of the problems—that you may suddenly come down with a fever.

The failing of the immunity screen has a lot to do with the recent return of the old killer, tuberculosis,

*The importance of the hypothalamus in immunity has been demonstrated repeatedly in experiments. If you stimulate a certain area of an animal's hypothalamus, its antibody output will rise. But if the same area is surgically removed, its immune reactions will be destroyed.

which not so long ago was considered virtually erad-
icated. Probably a third of the world's population, including many thousands of Americans, actually carry
live tuberculosis bacilli, but most of their immunity
screens are able to cope. Let the screen deteriorate,
however, and the bacilli multiply in their lungs. This
is why so many AIDS victims, as their immunity deteriorates—the characteristic of the dread disease—
contract TB.

ALLERGIES

People get sick not only when their resistance lowers,
but also when it rises too high. These are the people
with the inflammatory diseases like an allergy or arthritis—diseases in which the body is injured not by
some malevolent microbe, but by its own protective
devices, senselessly firing away at a harmless challenge, sometimes at no challenge at all.

This is indisputably true of allergy, still it remains
in many ways a mystifying affliction. One of the curious facts about the allergic reaction is that stress hormones in the form of drugs (cortisone, for example),
usually bring relief, yet stress itself, as experienced in
daily life, tends to make it worse. And allergies don't
respond to all invaders in the same fashion. The asthmatic reacts normally to chicken pox and measles. It
is only house dust, or pollen, or animal dander that
sets him gasping for breath.*

Plasma cells produce several different types of antibodies, and it is now known that one of them, Immunoglobulin E (IgE), is especially active in allergy. IgE not only
attacks the invading antigen, it also stimulates the body to

---

*However, a few people do react allergically to cold viruses, and
some doctors believe that tuberculosis symptoms are basically allergic.

release certain chemicals—histamine is one—which cause tissues to swell, mucus secretions to rise, and air passages in the lungs to contract. Perhaps further research into IgE will clear up the mystery of allergy.

For years, of course, some psychologists have been claiming that allergy is at heart an emotional disease. In many patients no physical antigen is discoverable, a situation that may be true of 50 percent of asthmatics. Allergists themselves say that in all probability an antigen does exist, and will be located eventually, when techniques of detection improve; but their case remains to be demonstrated. Meanwhile, psychologists have unearthed some interesting evidence to support their view.

A group headed by Dr. J. J. Groen, at a hospital in Amsterdam, for some years ran experiments on asthma. In one of these, a woman who was allergic to horses began to wheeze when merely shown a photograph of a horse. A second woman, hypersensitive to goldfish, reacted not only to a toy fish, but to an empty fish bowl. Still other patients were conditioned to respond allergically to ordinary uncontaminated air. For instance, a woman allergic to pollen inhaled alternating doses of pollen-laden air, room air and pure oxygen. After a number of such sessions she reached the point where the room air and even the oxygen brought on her asthma just as forcefully as the pollen did—in fact, just placing the mouthpiece of the inhalator between her lips could induce an attack.

In other words, some people who are irritated by a particular pollen are equally sensitive to the *idea* of the pollen.

An attack of asthma can be brought on not only by an idea but also by emotions that the patient has learned to connect with wheezing, coughing, or other allergic symptoms. Very often these emotions involve his or her parents. The parents of an allergic child tend to behave in a rather special way. They cannot greet an asthma attack in their child as calmly as they would a cold, or even a bout of pneumonia. It is more frightening—and it is also more avoidable. So they become bossy and overprotective. No, their son can't play baseball in the vacant lot with the other kids—doesn't he know there's ragweed down there? And he's got to go to bed earlier than his friends, because it's when he gets tired that his attacks are worse. Catching cold brings them on too, so he'd better wear his rubbers today—there's a 40 percent chance of rain.

The psychogenic view of allergy holds that the attitude of such parents is not so much a reaction to their child's allergy as it is a basic part of their personality; they are overprotective to start with, and this is one reason why he has become allergic. Whatever the etiology, the child reacts by becoming excessively dependent on the parents, but at the same time feels rebellious against them. These are the feelings that become connected with allergic attacks—so much so that when other circumstances arouse these feelings, an allergic attack may take place even if the physical antigen is absent.

The best cure for some severely asthmatic children is to send them away from home. In Holland before World War II, they were often sent to Switzerland, where their improvement was ascribed to the change of altitude. But when war came and foreign travel was no longer possible, doctors found they could get just as good results by sending these children to homes in a neighboring Dutch town. In these cases no steps were taken to desensitize the environment. The children simply got better—and it was noted that a letter from home might bring on the first real attack in months.

Many asthma patients find it hard to express their feelings. Their longing to be taken care of prevents them from acting rebellious, and their rebelliousness prevents them from acting dependent, so they can become almost immobilized emotionally. As a medical group they are notorious for their inability to weep. Some psychologists say an asthma attack is nothing but a suppressed cry for Mother, and it can often be broken up if the patient bursts into tears. Others feel it is more a protest against maternal domination—the patient's way of saying, "I feel smothered." Franz Alexander links asthma to the breath-holding habit common in some children—a device something like a hunger strike, to protest against the quality of maternal love.

In fact some "allergies" may not be true allergies at all—just a way of responding to anything that the patient finds disturbing, be it physical or psychological. Wolf and Wolff wrote: ". . . some people appear to be nasal reactors, especially prone to nasal swellings and obstruction from infection, atmospheric change, disturbing irritants, pollens, or to people and events in their lives which may also act as irritants."* Likewise, there is evidence that some colds are not really colds. Lawrence E. Hinkle and William N. Christenson studied twenty-four random women over a period of six months and found that a few of them "caught" cold far more often than could be explained by exposure to infection. Lab tests showed the presence of Asian flu virus in their blood at times, but these were not usually the times when their symptoms appeared. The symptoms appeared when the women were under emotional pressure.

RHEUMATOID ARTHRITIS

In rheumatoid arthritis, seemingly, the villain is inflammation pure and simple—no microbial agent or other invader has ever been identified with it, although

*Stewart Wolf and Harold G. Wolff, *Headaches: Their Nature and Treatment.* Boston, Little, 1953.

many doctors believe such an invader does exist and will some day be found. Again like allergy, rheumatoid arthritis is made worse by stress of all kinds, and yet it is relieved by taking cortisone or ACTH, the hormones the body puts forth in situations of acute stress. For these and other reasons, some doctors believe arthritis is at heart allergic.

But there are important differences between the two states. Most allergies attack organs that are relatively exposed: the digestive tract, the nose and lungs, the skin. Yet the joints are one of the best protected areas in the body.

Rheumatoid arthritis will be discussed further in the following chapter, "The Skeletal-Muscular System." It comes up here because so many investigators are coming to believe that the real villain is a specific derangement in some people's bodily defenses called auto-immunity. Auto-immunity has been implicated in a number of other serious ailments, ranging from ulcerative colitis to schizophrenia—and, to complete the circle, possibly even allergy itself.

Auto-immunity is a condition in which the immune system fails in its most important single task—the distinction between self and not-self—and starts manufacturing antibodies against the patient's own tissue. Just why and how this happens has not yet been discovered. Some think mutation is involved—noncancerous changes in certain body cells, with a consequent change in their antigens.

Auto-immunity may also occur when an invading microbe happens to possess antigens that are almost identical to the antigens of the patient's own body tissue. In rheumatic fever, for instance, the streptococcus antigen may so closely resemble certain protein molecules within the heart valves that antibodies manufactured against the first will also attack the second.

A third possibility has to do with the antigen-antibody complexes often found in the blood of patients with auto-immune diseases. Here is a situation where antibody attacks antigen but fails to destroy it—probably because antibody production is somewhat deficient. It is possible that these clumps of antigen-antibody become, in effect, new antigens, and the body fights back the only way it knows how. In the blood of three out of four rheumatoid arthritis patients a substance is found known as the rheumatoid factor. It appears to consist of two antibodies—one presumably against some unidentified invader, the second against the anti-invader antibody. These persist indefinitely. Presumably the invader itself is harmless, and the pain and crippling are wholly caused by the immune reaction.

Interestingly, among patients with ulcerative colitis, another disease that may involve auto-immune mechanisms, 15 percent also suffer from a mild form of arthritis, which usually disappears if the colitis clears up.

CANCER

In cancer the body also fails in its task of surveillance—the task of recognizing an enemy within its gates—but with reverse results. Here foe is mistaken for friend, and a deadly enemy is allowed to live and multiply inside the body without interference.

Cancerous mutations, it is now believed, are a regular occurrence in the lives of perfectly healthy people, who never know it because their immune systems destroy the mutant cell before it can multiply. But every now and then, in a certain individual, at a certain point in time, this reaction fails to take place. The mutant cell, despite its new antigens, survives, and gradually multiplies, and becomes a tumor, and the person goes to his doctor and discovers he has cancer.

How does a cell become cancerous in the first place? What exactly is a mutation?

A mutation is a change in the hereditary material

within an originally normal cell. The individual cells of the body, like the individual person whom they comprise, have a set of genetic characteristics which they pass on, through the DNA of the cell nucleus, to succeeding cells. These muscle cells reproduce muscle cells, just as ten-fingered parents reproduce ten-fingered children. Once in a great while, however, a nine-fingered baby is born, and this is because of a mutation in the cells of the very early embryo.

Many physical agents cause mutations. Chemicals can cause them; so can injuries and burns; so can X-ray, ultraviolet light, and ultrasonic agitation. And so can viruses.

A virus is the smallest and simplest organism known—in fact it only barely qualifies as an organism at all. You can take a little glass bottle, fill it with a few million viruses, put a stopper on it and store it on a shelf for fifty years, and you might as well be storing a handful of sand: inside that bottle absolutely nothing will happen, no intake of food or air, no output of waste, no reproduction, no death. If at the end of fifty years you pull out the stopper and release the viruses into the presence of living cells, then, and only then will they come to life of a sort. A virus is a kind of parasite, but like no other parasite. Its only known function is reproduction, and it can only reproduce inside a living cell. It does this by taking over the DNA of the cell nucleus and forcing it to serve the needs of the virus rather than of the cell—and the sole need of the virus is the reproduction of other viruses. Finally the cell bursts, releasing all these new viruses into the body, where they proceed to attack yet other cells and repeat the whole cycle.

Viruses are to blame for such assorted diseases as measles, polio, hepatitis and most colds, and they can also cause cancer—definitely, in animals, and most probably in humans as well. This is hardly surprising. If a virus attacks the living cell by attacking its DNA, and if DNA is the material that passes hereditary traits from parent cell to child cell, then it is only logical to expect mutations to result. And cellular mutation is the single basic fact about cancer.

Mutations induced by viruses are more dramatic than those caused by other forces, such as chemicals or radiation. A viral cancer is highly antigenic, and normally provokes a strong counterattack from the lymphocytes. If this counterattack is weakened, however, by stress or some other factor, viral cancers survive and begin to grow. They grow faster than chemical cancers.

What makes a tumor grow? Or why do some tumors fail to grow? Some individual cancer cells, even if they survive the attack of antibodies, remain dormant for long spells—some for a lifetime, others for a period of years before they suddenly begin to multiply. No one is sure why this dormant stage is so common, but it is probably because of the immune system. Although unable to destroy the cells outright, it is still capable of controlling their numbers.

And probably a sudden lowering of these immune defenses is what makes a long dormant cancer begin to grow.

In his book, *Cancer, the Wayward Cell,** Dr. Victor Richards points out that cancer cells do not actually reproduce all that fast. The real problem is that their reproduction rate is greater than their death rate. In normal cells these two rates are balanced—probably through a device known as contact inhibition. A normal cell does not reproduce when it is snugly surrounded by fellow cells; reproduction happens only if one or more of the other cells dies and disappears.

*Berkeley: University of California Press, 1972.

Electrical impulses may be involved—and it is known that cancer cells are highly resistant to electrical charges.

Another difference between cancer cells and normal cells is that normal cells are differentiated—that is, each type of cell has a certain function to perform, and a certain structure suited to that function. Thus a bone cell is very different from a muscle cell, so much so that under a microscope the bone cell of a human looks more like the bone cell of a mouse than like some other kind of cell from the human body.

One of the peculiarities of cancer cells is that they are not differentiated in this fashion. They are what scientists call de-differentiated. In fact, in many ways they behave like the original group of cells in the first few hours of an embryo's life, just after conception and before different types of tissue begin to form. The sole purpose of such embryonic cells is, of course, rapid growth. They neither contract muscles, nor secrete hormones, nor manufacture blood, nor perform any other specialized task. What they do is multiply. In an embryo such cells begin to mature and acquire their own identity within a few days. But in cancer this doesn't happen. A tumor not only fails to develop special functions to serve the body, the way normal cells do, but as it gets larger it begins to compete with normal cells for space and fuel, until eventually it takes over and destroys vital organs, and the body dies, tumor and all.

Stress helps to cause cancer because it depresses the immune response, the body's only real means of defending itself against malignant cells. One way it does this is through the action of the adrenal cortex hormones, which particularly affect the T-lymphocytes. Searching out foreign antigens in the body is one of the tasks of these T-lymphocytes, and significantly they measure at low levels in the tissues of most cancer patients.

But body reactions quite unconnected with immunity may go on to promote metastasis: the spreading of cancer from its original site to other organs. Metastasis takes place when cancer cells break away from a tumor, enter the blood stream, travel to a new area and become implanted there. Surgery sometimes can actually initiate this process, by causing a tumor to shed cells, and the same thing may happen because of muscular responses to stress, such as chronic spasms in the colon or lungs. Dr. George F. Solomon of Stanford University also believes that the increased coagulability of the blood, a normal reaction to stress, causes deposits of fibrin to form on the walls of blood vessels which may snag passing cancer cells. The cells then take up residence and begin growing into surrounding tissues.

Is it stress in general that makes people cancer prone, or is it a particular kind of stress? No one is really sure, but during the past hundred and fifty years numerous physicians have called attention to a distinctive state of mind in their cancer patients. Some have called it melancholy; others hopelessness, or despair, or deep-seated disappointment. Often it is associated with the recent loss of a relative or close friend.

In the early 1950s a clinical psychologist, Dr. Lawrence LeShan, of the Institute of Applied Biology, decided to investigate this state of mind. Over a period of twelve years he tested four hundred and fifty adult cancer patients, forty-five of whom received intensive individual psychotherapy. What he came up with is a portrait of a personality as individual, certainly as haunting, as any in medical literature.

This is how Dr. LeShan described his typical cancer patient:

Early in life, apparently during the first seven years, damage was done to the child's developing ability to relate. Often this was accentuated by a physical event, such as the loss of a parent, the death of a sibling, or something of this sort. From his experience at this time, the child learned to feel that emotional relationships brought pain and desertion. Loneliness was his doom. In the usual manner of children, this was attributed to some fault of his own rather than to the result of accidental forces. Guilt and self-condemnation were the inevitable response.

The traumatic situation or crisis had not the kind of timing and intensity which would be likely to produce obvious neurotic symptoms or to prepare the individual for psychosis in the event of later stress. From a surface viewpoint, he managed to adjust adequately to his environment. However, the orientation that social relationships were dangerous and that there was something very much wrong with him, persisted and colored his life. Little real energy was invested in relationships. His cathexes to other people were essentially superficial and no matter what he achieved, his basic feelings of failure predominated. To use Kierkegaard's phrase, he was "in despair of being himself. . . ."

Sometime in his development, usually in our cases in late adolescence or early adulthood, a situation arose that offered an opportunity for relating to others; a perceived chance to end the deep loneliness he felt. This possibility seemed somehow "safe." Over a period of time, a period of slow and cautious experimentation, he began to pour his energies into this channel. The feelings of isolation and "lostness," the deep loneliness were greatly, but never completely, eased by this relationship. A tremendous amount of psychic and usually physical energy was poured into it. The cathexis gave a meaning to life. For a period ranging from one year to over forty, they had a meaningful existence and a channel into which to pour their energy.

Sometimes it was a job with a role for which they seemed particularly well adapted and which they enjoyed. Sometimes as a spouse, a parent or both, they found a way of life that brought them closer to satisfaction and relatedness than they had ever dreamed was possible. They still found it difficult to express or defend their own wishes, but in the interest of their group or of the relationship, they could act very strongly.

For a shorter or longer period, life continued on this plane. Then the blow fell. Circumstances brought an end to the relationship; their role was lost. Job retirement was forced on them, a spouse died, children grew up, became independent and no longer needed them. The immediate reaction varies. Some made desperate efforts to find substitute relationships. They tried to obtain new jobs, to make new friends, to find a new group, only to fail. Others were crushed by the blow. From a superficial view, all continued to "adjust." They continued to function and went about their daily business, but there was no more meaning and hope to their lives. Nothing gave them real satisfaction. It seemed to them as though the thing they had expected and feared all their lives—utter isolation and rejection—was now their eternal doom. . . .

The early fantasy of something being basically wrong with them, something that made them unacceptable to others, returned in full force. Their energy level declined, because now there was no meaningful channel for its expression, and the decline was soon felt. The color and zest went out of life. At some time from six months to eight years after the crucial cathexis was lost, the first symptoms of cancer appeared in the cases we observed.*

Dr. LeShan also found a high statistical correlation between malignancy and specific life events in these patients—for instance, the birth of a younger brother or sister before the patient had reached his second birthday, or an unhappy marriage, particularly in

*Lawrence LeShan, "An Emotional Life History Pattern Associated with Neoplastic Disease," from the Annals of the New York Academy of Sciences, 1966.

women who developed cancer of the cervix. But what impressed him most strongly was this more generalized life pattern of disappointment, loneliness and loss of hope.

One of his patients said to him: "You know how it is with a house with no insulation and with cracks in the walls? The more heat you put in, the more leaks out. You can never get it warm. I always knew that was how it was with me in life. I had to keep putting and putting out and there was never any reflection back toward me. If I was going to get warm inside, I'd have to do it alone, and no matter how much you do, you can't do that."

Another said: "Last time I hoped, and look what happened. As soon as my defenses were down, of course it happened and I was left alone again. I'll never hope again. It's too much."

And a third used to say: "If the rock drops on the egg—poor egg. If the egg drops on the rock—poor egg."

CHAPTER 4

The Skeletal-Muscular System: Backache, Tension Headache, Arthritis, the Accident-prone

Watching passersby on a busy street from a bus window, you can learn quite a bit about them, even if you can't see their eyes or hear what they are saying. You learn it from the way they move.

A nine-year-old breaks into an exuberant run. He's just been released from school.

A woman in her twenties passes confidently along, shoulders easy, handbag swinging, the trace of a smile on her lips—a person who knows where she is going.

Half a block behind, but gaining, comes a man with big shoulders and a heavy stride. His arms don't move as he walks, elbows back, hands clenched, staring into the faces of the people who pass him. They do not return his glance. He is an aggressive man, an angry man, and they don't want to get involved with him.

At the corner, waiting to cross, stands a girl of fourteen. The light turns green, and she darts into the street; then an instant later jumps back to the curb to escape a turning car, bumping into the person behind her; flustered, she suddenly bounds across to the opposite curb. There she remembers something—and all at once her posture undergoes a change. She lets her shoulders go. Even her eyelids lower. She begins to move in an indolent glide, smoothly and efficiently traversing the pavement, her face impassive. She has learned this way of moving, perhaps from another girl, perhaps from a movie star.

These people are all using their bones and muscles

to accomplish something, even if it is only a walk in the afternoon sunshine. At the same time they are using their equipment to express something about themselves. Sometimes they are saying what they feel; sometimes what they would like to feel. Most of the time they are saying a little of both.

A smile is a muscular act. So is a frown. Everyone expresses feelings muscularly. But some people do it more than others: babies and young children, and also certain adults. Often, though not always, these are people who find it a little hard to express themselves in words. Included are many athletes, carpenters, actors and dancers, both professional and amateur, as well as quite a few people with chronic medical problems. This is not surprising. Obviously a quarterback exposes himself to risks that a file clerk does not.

But it isn't quite that simple. Actually, of the many people who suffer from ailments involving the skeletal-muscular system, only some are strong physical-action types. Others appear to be almost the opposite. The truth is that muscles and bones are used not only to express feelings, but to *repress* them.

BACKACHE AND TENSION HEADACHE

"Sitting tight" describes the state of the typical patient with chronic functional backache. His problem most usually is not that he lifts too many heavy loads or overdoes at the gym. On the contrary. During World War II Doctors Barbara Stimson, Sonja Weber and Hans Kraus started a back clinic at Columbia-Presbyterian Hospital in New York, and through X-rays, laboratory procedures and exercise tests made a startling discovery. Some 80 percent of their patients were suffering from muscular deficiency, pure and simple.

A muscle is like many other parts of the body—it

isn't normally injured by use, even by a great deal of use. Exercise strengthens muscles, partly because it makes them more flexible. This flexibility is important. Muscles contract when they are performing a job. But when the job is finished they should know how to relax. The difference in the length of a muscle between a state of rest and a state of exertion is one measure of its efficiency.

When people feel like acting but don't allow themselves to act, their muscles remain tensed in readiness, sometimes for months or years at a time, immobilized into a state of semi-contraction even during sleep. If this condition goes on long enough, the muscle gradually loses it elasticity, and with it much of its effectiveness. Such a muscle *is* overused. It never gets a chance to rest. And in order to perform even a minor action the overused muscle must contract extra hard to make up for its permanently shortened condition.

This is chronic muscle spasm, by far the commonest cause of trouble for people who suffer the miseries of recurrent backache. What are these people like?

At heart most of them are *action* types. Action is their natural way of achieving things, of solving problems and of expressing anger, and many come from a childhood studded by temper tantrums and fighting. But in adult life this approach does not seem to have paid off, and they have ceased to trust it. They are competitive people who feel they are not getting "their own," resentful of those they feel are to blame—often a boss, or a husband or wife—and deeply unsure of what to do about it all. Angry and apprehensive, they cannot take action, yet they are constantly on guard and ready to act. Their muscles are often tense all over the body. But it is the muscles of the back that usually feel the strain because they are the most vulnerable. Evolutionarily, we are descendants of four-legged animals; our erect posture is a relatively recent development, and our back muscles are still in the process of catching up. They are supposed to get help from the stomach muscles and hip flexors, but these are so weakened by today's sedentary living that they often have little to contribute.

Chronic muscle tension can hurt in other areas besides the back. Some people get toothaches from clenching their jaws habitually—a muscular exertion which, if it persists long enough, can also affect the bones in the gum and lead to early tooth loss. A more common affliction is the tension headache. Here it is the muscles of the neck and scalp that cause the trouble. Most people come down with this kind of headache at some point in their lives, but some have it regularly and a few get headaches that persist for a year or longer. Often, like backache patients, they are restless, unsure people constantly poised for action but unable to trust their own impulses.

One of the problems in both backache and tension headache is the cyclical nature of the pain. Muscle tension makes you hurt; then hurting makes you tense your muscles further, which makes you hurt still more.

It isn't easy to relax when you hurt. This is why some doctors give tranquilizers, along with aspirin, to a headache patient. Heat and massage help a sore back because they help the muscles let go.

ARTHRITIS

Muscles and bones are the sturdy workhorses of the human body, tough, energetic, and quick to recover if injured. But crucial to their operations is a more delicate piece of machinery: the joint. A professional football player knows this well. A broken finger or a pulled calf muscle is nothing in his life. It is his knees that he worries about.

When a joint becomes inflamed, the condition is called arthritis. Injury can cause arthritis; so can infection; so can ordinary wear and tear over years of living. Most elderly people are at least mildly arthritic, especially if they are overweight. Their condition is called osteoarthritis.

The real crippler, however, is rheumatoid arthritis, a disease that attacks people in the prime of life. Sometimes it stays a year or two and then mysteriously vanishes. Usually it settles in for good, slowly spreading pain and stiffness from one joint to another. In severe cases scar tissue forms at the adjoining bone ends and eventually turns into bone itself, freezing the joint into permanent immobility. Rheumatoid arthritis can be treated, but no one knows how to cure it. No one even knows its cause.

Like many chronic diseases, it may have a number of causes all working together—one of which may well be a faulty immune response in the body (see pp. 73–75), another of which is probably stress. As we know, stress does affect the immunologic system. In addition, there is some evidence that stress affects arthritis more directly.

For years, physicians have been struck both by the fact that stress problems seem to make arthritis worse, and by certain similarities in the way many arthritis patients behave. Often they are rather rigid, domineering people, somewhat shy socially, who early in life learned to take out their feelings in aggressive physical action. They play tennis. They swim. They garden. They go for long, vigorous walks—and it is hard for an ordinary person to keep up. Like the backache victim, they associate physical activity with the expression of aggression and hostility. Unlike him, they have found it a satisfying and on the whole trustworthy outlet for these emotions.

Nevertheless, hostility is a problem for them, and often it hinges on sexual roles. In rheumatoid arthritis, three out of four patients are women, and most of them resent it. Though they usually marry and raise families, they tend to select rather passive husbands whom they can keep under control, and they are the same with their children. This does not mean they mistreat their families. Often they are unusually solicitous—fine cooks and tireless household managers, magnanimous and even in their way loving, so long as they remain in control. In fact, they are somewhat masochistic about it all. By knocking themselves out caring for husband and children, they relieve not only their inner hostility, but also the feeling of guilt that this hostility produces. Theirs is a pattern of life aimed at balancing these two emotions, and sometimes it goes on working indefinitely.

But sometimes it doesn't. The husband, feeling vaguely threatened, begins to assert himself. The children grow older and rebel against all that care. Sexual relations, always difficult, come to seem an outright humiliation. With the passage of years, too, the person's physical energy begins to dwindle, and with it her accepted emotional outlets. She's no longer up to three sets of tennis, and repainting the downstairs ceilings leaves her worn out and depressed. In other words, one reason she gets sick is not that she expresses her feelings through physical labor and exercise, but because physical labor and exercise no longer work for her.

Rheumatoid factor is an element found in the blood of most patients with rheumatoid arthritis. Interestingly, it is sometimes found in the blood of healthy people as well—including, at times, athletes after a hard game. In 1965 Drs. George F. Solomon and R. H. Moos published a study comparing a group of rheumatoid arthritis patients with various healthy relatives. Some of these healthy relatives possessed the rheumatoid factor, and some did not. Those without the factor remained healthy despite the usual assortment of psychological problems common to the general population. But the striking thing about those who did possess the rheumatoid factor was their sound emotional balance. Often they resembled their arthritic relatives in taking a physically active approach to life—and often from similar motives. But in their case the approach was working well for them. Solomon and Moos concluded by suggesting that stress alone doesn't produce arthritis, and neither does the rheumatoid factor, but perhaps the two together do.

A number of physicians suspect that muscle tension of the sort involved in back trouble and tension headaches also contributes to arthritis. Franz Alexander noted that the onset of the disease was often preceded by attacks of muscular pain. And it has been shown that arthritics under emotional pressure do respond with abnormal muscle tension, particularly in the muscles closest to the afflicted joints. It is possible that this tension injures the joints in small ways, making them more susceptible to disease, or even altering their chemical make-up and thereby arousing an immune reaction within the body.

This possibility has been discussed in the preceding chapter. At any rate it seems clear that there is more to the disease than simple mechanical strain. Rheumatoid arthritis affects the whole body, not just the joints. Among its symptoms are fever, anemia, and reduced blood flow to the extremities. Perhaps more important, in rheumatoid arthritis the body loses collagen, a basic element in all connective tissue, resulting in weight loss, brittle bones, loose ligaments, and a withering of the skin. Normally collagen makes up a third of the body's total weight. No one knows how it is formed, but pituitary and sex hormones both appear to influence its manufacture.

ACCIDENTS

In medical research, when you decide to investigate a disease the customary procedure is to get together a group of people who are afflicted, plus a group of people who are not, and then to compare the two groups, the aim being to weed out irrelevant factors. Thus if 64 percent of the sick people excrete chemical X in their urine but only 8 percent of the control group do, then chemical X is worth looking into. But if the percentages are more or less equal, there probably is little point in going further.

Back in the 1930s when Flanders Dunbar undertook her massive study of psychogenic factors in the patient population at Columbia-Presbyterian, she chose accident patients, primarily fracture cases, as her control group. Her logic seemed sound. An accident by definition is a coincidence, the result not of causative forces, mental or physical, at work in the body, but of random chance. Before long, however, Dr. Dunbar began to wonder; and by the time her study was complete, she was ready with another definition. In the typical fracture patient, she asserted, the statistics run much too high to be explained by chance; accidents are not necessarily accidental; psychogenic forces often *are* at work. And the concept of the accident-prone received major new support.

For some years this concept flourished and much research was done in its support, some of it perhaps a little too enthusiastic. In any event, a reaction has set in in recent years, and controversy once more surrounds the subject. To the layman much of this controversy often seems a kind of semantic quibble. Are people accident prone, or merely accident liable? Is accident-proneness a basic and permanent quality of the personality, or a temporary state induced by worry or some other distracting emotion? Aren't some people simply unlucky?

Perhaps the only safe thing to say is that there are accidents and accidents. I know of a ten-year-old boy who is forever getting injured, one of those scrappy, enthusiastic children who never seem to learn. Last summer he went away to camp for the first time, and two days after his departure his parents received a phone call from the nurse—Jeff had had "a little tumble" out of a tree, and broken his arm. It had been set by a doctor, though, and he was fine: a brave little fellow. Ten days later the second call came—he had stepped on a rusty nail in the stables: was he up to date on his booster shots? Then on the following night came the third call, this one from Jeff himself.

"Mom, I'm in the hospital."

"Oh Jeff! What have you done now!"

With a certain pride he answered: "I got struck by lightning."

It was true. During a thunderstorm, he had picked up the camp phone to call home about something, when lightning hit the lines and passed through him, knocking him cold: the next thing he knew he was in the emergency room having his pants cut off him—lightning had welded the zipper together. He was okay now, but would she please send him another pair of pants?

In short, even in the accident-prone, accidents can be accidental. Jeff recovered swiftly and went on to sprain a finger and cut a leg (three stitches), before returning home at the end of August, two inches taller. It had been a great summer, he said.

The statistics may be arguable but the fact remains: people like Jeff exist. How do they get that way?

It sometimes seems that the accident-prone constitute not one but two groups of people, with certain overlapping traits but also a number of distinctions. Both groups are doers—busy, on the go, interested in challenging and mastering their physical environment. Exposure is an important element in accidents. Jeff will do anything on a dare, and is proud of it.

He is proud, too, of his courage in the face of injury. He hasn't really cried from pain since he was seven, that time the doctor probed for gravel in his wounded palm. He doesn't enjoy pain, but he enjoys rising above it, rather in the same way he enjoys recovering from his various injuries. He has a sense of mastering adversity, even perhaps of some power over fate itself. Look at all the things that have happened to him. Yet he still goes on, every year taller and tougher and more capable. He must be made of very strong stuff.*

---

* Jerry Kramer, a famous lineman who played for the Green Bay Packers till his retirement in 1969, was accident prone and found an expressive career for the tendency. In the appendix of his book, *Farewell to Football*, (World Publishing Company, 1969) he lists the major mishaps of his life (the minor ones were too numerous to include) as follows:

Age 3 — Dropped axe and fell on it, cutting chin and throat. Stitches.

Age 7 — Fell out of tree. Cut arm open. Stitches.

Age 14 — Caught T-shirt in turning screw of lathe. Ripped out fist-sized chunk of right side. Stitches.

Age 15 — Accidentally shot right arm and side with double-barrel 10-gauge shotgun. Wound required four operations, skin grafts, and plastic surgery over the next few years.

Age 17 — Ran into sharp board while chasing calf in pasture. Seven-and-one-half-inch long, three-quarter-inch thick splinter penetrated groin and lodged in large muscle near spine. Major operation.

Age 18 — Brain concussion sustained in football game.

Age 19 — Operation for suspected chipped vertebra in neck.

Age 20 — Brain concussion sustained in football game.

Age 23 — Brain concussion and detached retina of left eye sustained in game against Los Angeles Rams in 1960. Operation to correct detached retina delayed until after season.

Age 24 — Two bones in left ankle separated and ligaments severely strained during game with Minnesota Vikings in 1961. Left shin also broken but not discovered until 1963.

A psychologist might suggest that underneath Jeff's feelings lies an unspoken fear of helplessness, of mutilation, of death, and perhaps also certain inner doubts about his manliness; and that Jeff fights down these fears and doubts by acting aggressive and daring. This is true of some people, obviously, although hard to believe in the case of this young boy. However, there is no question that he gets a certain heartening reassurance out of all his repeated recoveries, the feeling that he leads a charmed life, and that whatever he feels like doing he might as well go ahead and do because it will come out all right in the end. When he gets old enough to drive, this is the kind of confidence that may lead to tragedy. It is the same kind of confidence that is fostered by alcohol, and is a major reason why an automobile often becomes a lethal weapon in the hands of a drinker.

You can fault Jeff for behaving a little unrealistically, then, but you can't fault him for much else. And in fact the mores of his society actively support his way of life. He is aggressive; he is brave; he takes chances. We admire people like that. We admire Troy Aikman on Sunday afternoons as he sets up to pass, with that defensive line coming at him.

Jeff is one kind of accident-repeater. There is a second kind, driven by somewhat darker motives. Both

---

Age 25 — Two ribs broken during game with San Francisco 49ers in 1962.

Age 28 — Operation for tumor on liver. Emergency colostomy. Postoperative pneumonia. Six-and-one-half hour operation in lower left abdominal area during which four slivers of wood (that had been lodged for eleven years) were removed. Operation to close colostomy. Operation for hernia near breastbone.

Age 32 — Right thumb broken in game against Atlanta Falcons. Ligaments of right knee stretched in game against Detroit Lions. Nerves in shoulder pinched in later game.

kinds are impulsive people, willing to take chances, with an aggressive approach to life. Perhaps the difference lies in the quality of their aggression. Jeff is scrappy and hyperactive. But some accident-repeaters are angry. Sometimes their anger is quite evident. You can spot them on the expressway through your rearview mirror, and you quickly ease over into the right lane, grateful to let them zoom past and out of your life.

But sometimes the anger is veiled, and sometimes it is very deeply hidden, both from the world and from the person himself. This seemed to be the case with most of Dr. Dunbar's fracture patients—a group that at first glance seemed characterized by easy sociability and a happy-go-lucky air. Paradoxically, these patients in many ways took unusually good care of themselves—the kind of people who go in for sports, diets, and body-building—and in fact their general health was excellent. Almost all were enthusiastic athletes, but their injuries rarely occurred on a playing field. Instead it was a momentary and inexplicable clumsiness—at the head of a flight of stairs, or stepping off a curb—that brought them to the hospital. The question was: Why did it keep happening?

The statistics led Dr. Dunbar to investigate further, and eventually to uncover a mass of evidence. Beneath the amiable exterior, most of these people were actually deeply hostile—and early in life they had shown it. Seventy percent had been difficult children, with such problems as stealing and truancy. This was true despite their harsh upbringing—or perhaps because of it. Actually, they were punished frequently and sometimes savagely, but with little effect. "I would take my licking and holler, and then go out and do it anyway," one patient recalled.

Defiance of authority was the name of the game—overt and outspoken in childhood, later buried beneath that complex cover of easy cheerfulness, but still operative. These people could not stand having anyone over them for long. Many had quit school before they graduated, and even during the depression they were forever quitting jobs. They also quit marriages with unusual ease. Yet they did not seem to want to assume power themselves. They were reluctant to have children, and showed little ambition to climb the organizational ladder at work, or even to aim for a general goal in life. Authority was not something to acquire, but something to get away from.

But they could never get away from it altogether, and it was when this basic problem in their lives came to a head in feelings of hostility and resentment that the accidents usually occurred. Guilt, too, was involved. Possibly through their punishment-studded childhoods they acquired a permanent need for the whippings of an angry father. One woman said of her accidental fall, "Well, God brought me to my knees just as my parents used to do."

Accident patients do punish themselves. Often they also punish other people—the spouse who will have to care for them during convalescence, the employer who keeps the salary going without any return in labor (or who may well get slapped with a lawsuit if the accident occurred at work). Almost a third of Dr. Dunbar's fracture patients were legal compensation cases.

Many accidents, of course, punish perfectly innocent bystanders, along with the perpetrator, and some accidents kill, especially when an automobile is involved. Between the impulse toward self-punishment and the impulse toward suicide, the line is very hazy. The same is true for suicide and murder. According to Karl Menninger's famous dictum, a suicidal person wants three things: to kill; to be killed; and to die. Hostility, intense and unrelieved, underlies all of these three aims, and when this hostility goes unacknowledged, a car can be a more appropriate weapon than a gun.

Automobile advertising does not help matters. A car in our society is a symbol of power, not only over distance, but more importantly, over other drivers. The cars themselves are named Cougar, Jaguar, Mustang, and certainly our highways are often jungles, ruled by those qualities we cannot help admiring—competitiveness; pluck; taking chances. And these qualities are not really diminished by another well-known feature of modern transportation, the traffic jam. The king of the jungle may find himself inching along with all the worms, but you can be sure that when the road finally opens he's going to make up for it, particularly if he is a chronically angry person, or if he is undergoing some crisis in his life. Twenty percent of all fatal car accidents involve drivers who have suffered an upsetting experience within six hours before the crash, and one out of three accident victims was depressed.

PART THREE

How It Happens:
The Pathways of Stress

CHAPTER 5

How the Mind Handles Stress

From the preceding chapters it may seem that the equipment people possess for dealing with stress is quite faulty, full of holes and leaks. Let's take a closer look.

Perhaps the first thing to be said is that this equipment goes together to make a unified whole, and in charge of that whole is the mind. In the words of Franz Alexander, "The fact that the mind rules the body is, in spite of its neglect by biology and medicine, the most fundamental fact we know about the process of life." It is in the mind that we confront a problem, not in the stomach or the joints—though the mind may call on the stomach for a solution, or may pass the problem on to the joints if solution fails.

A problem presents itself to the mind in three stages. We perceive it (we need to cross the street, say), analyze it (we study the flow of traffic), and reach our decision. Finally we take action, we cross. Does all this sound too simple, too logical? Yes it does, for this is not the way people behave when they are under pressure. Logic may constitute the first line of attack, but behind logic lies a whole battery of emotional artillery. These emotions are supposed to provide supportive fire, and they do, but to carry the military analogy further, they are also capable of hitting their own front line troops in the process. And if the battle goes badly and defeat threatens, the emotions may take over altogether, sometimes with disastrous results.

What are these emotions, and what do they do to attack our problems? How do they help, and how do they hinder us?

They help because they signal the problem to us, and because they goad us into action.

They hinder, because the action they goad us into is usually physical action, and in the modern world physical action seldom solves the real problems.

An accountant is refused a raise in salary, and his first furious impulse is to hit his employer. But what does he really do?

What do *you* do in this kind of situation?

First of all, yes, you perceive. You watch the boss smile in that cool way of his, and your ears take in his words: "Warren, you're in accounting, you know the situation as well as I do: Unfortunately, a raise is out of the question this year." You perceive all right—and the emotions start to churn. The faint sweat of fear that accompanied you into his office is adumbrated by anger. And in fear and anger you pass on to the stage of analysis: "I'll bet he raised Sevringhaus! I *know* he raised Thompson! He never has recognized all I do for this lousy outfit!" The problem thus analyzed, you start looking for solutions. First thing tomorrow morning you'll check out the situation at Cohn & Mathison. They wanted you a year ago, didn't they? But do they still? God, all that money you've got tied up in the retirement fund! Oh God, are you going to have to start sucking around like Sevringhaus does? And so forth and so on, all your thoughts permeated with fear and anger.

One function of these emotions is, as pointed out, informational; like the sensation of pain in a physical injury, they're telling you that something has gone wrong. And like pain, they are unpleasant; and this unpleasantness acts as a spur, urging you to correct the situation. What is unfortunate, however, is that these emotions may do nothing to support your only real means for solution: clear thinking. You haven't even allowed yourself to consider the possibility that rankles the worst: What if you don't deserve a raise? What if you're not worth it? The emotions have an older and simpler prescription: knock the bastard down and don't let him up again until he promises you the raise.

Warren's emotions are not only telling him what to do, they also are taking steps that will enable him to act with maximum effect, chiefly by informing the endocrine system that a battle is at hand. Adrenaline from the adrenal medulla and glucagon and insulin from the pancreas flood him with a surge of surplus energy. Assorted other hormones constrict his arteries, raise his heart beat, and drain the blood out of his skin (causing him to bleed less should he sustain injuries during the melee).

With these processes going on inside his body, is it surprising that Warren finds it hard to be rational? Indeed, he's up against not one problem but two: the problem of the problem, so to speak, and the problem of his response to the problem—and the second of these is the more immediate. His best hope of success may be to go home first and split a few logs with a good, heavy sledge; and then, and only then, sit down and start figuring out how to approach Cohn & Mathison.

Physiologically, the brain is the organ of the mind. But what we know about the brain does not yet account for all that we know about the mind, and so in order to describe the mind's operations we have evolved the science of psychology. When we talk psychology, we talk not of the cerebrum and brain stem, but of the conscious and the unconscious, the id, the ego, and the superego. These are the classical Freudian concepts, although today they are the subject of dispute or modification by some schools of psychology (see Part Four).

If the mind rules the body, it is the ego that rules the mind, according to Freud, and to the extent that it rules firmly and realistically, the individual person possesses that ill-defined but undoubted blessing known as mental health. This kind of rule is not easy to maintain, for the ego must contend with the area of instinct and passion, which Freud christened the id, and also with the area of conscience, which he named the superego. To put it very roughly, instinct says "I must!"; conscience says "I mustn't!" The ego says, "Let's get together and work something out." The ego not only handles the conflicts between the id and the superego, but between the inner self and the outside worlds of society and of nature. The ego, in short, is the commanding general of the human organism. In this connection it is also the part of the mind that learns from experience. It remembers. It anticipates. It plans.

What are these inner demands that the ego must deal with and balance? Freud wrote at length about the sexual drive and the aggressive drive, the pleasure principle and the death wish. But perhaps for our purposes we can speak more pragmatically. People in their daily lives all need such things as food, drink, shelter, rest; success and power; communion with other people; sex; intellectual and physical growth; a sense of good and evil; a sense of beauty; a little fun; and a sense of self, a sense of the meaning of one's life. A person will lead a satisfying life if he can more or less fill all these needs. And in order to do so, he resorts to two basic forms of human behavior. One is aggression. The other is dependency.

Psychologically speaking, an act of aggression is not necessarily an act of war—aggression is not limited to hostility. Perhaps it is best defined as independent self-assertion, which can be either constructive or destructive. Spanking your children is aggressive. So is building a house. So is holding up a gas station. So is working your way through college. It is the do-it-yourself approach to problems.

Dependency, of course, is the get-someone-else-to-do-it approach, but it almost always involves some admixture of aggression. An infant doesn't have to go out and find its own food, it is fed by its mother, but it does have to cry first, and crying is an aggressive act. Pure dependency exists only in the womb—and perhaps on your birthday, when people give you presents simply because you exist.

Aggression and dependency, then, are the ways to get what we feel we need in life, and as a result they are so important to us that in a sense they become needs themselves. Freud considered aggression one of the two basic drives, along with sex, and modern psychiatrists are always talking about dependency needs. It is worth remembering, however, that fundamentally they are means to an end, not ends themselves.

Individual people, through experience, sometimes learn that one form of behavior works better for them than the other, and so we end up with some people who are mainly aggressive and some who are mainly dependent. We acquire these traits through the long years of childhood, sometimes only to discover that they don't work so well in adult life, and by that time it is hard to change. This is the case with many backache patients, who as children learned to get what they wanted by being scrappy and aggressive, but now can find no outlet for their ingrained impulses except through painful muscular tension.

In fact all of us, every day of our lives, use both aggressive behavior and dependent behavior to satisfy our needs, and we often employ them simultaneously. Warren the accountant is no exception. Perhaps he shows dependency in trying to persuade his employer to give him more money. But it is aggressive of him to demand a raise (as he knows—it took several days to work up his courage), and of course he has to be somewhat aggressive to work at the job in return for the salary.

So he uses a combination of aggression and dependency—and he fails. He has, of course, other options, Colin & Mathison for one. But say he fails there too, say he can't get a higher salary anywhere. What then?

Then the only thing he can do is try to reduce his needs—move into a smaller house, and inform his children that if they want to go to college they will have to take out a loan or work their way through. He will also have to alter his definition of himself—to get used to the melancholy idea that he is worth thirty thousand dollars a year, but no more; that he is not, after all, one of those brilliant and indispensable fellows with an ever-expanding future that he had always vaguely supposed.

These changes are hard on Warren, and it is not surprising that they are accompanied by changes in his aggression-dependency balance. Because a major problem in life continues unsolved, he will begin to resemble what Dr. George Engel calls the helpless-hopeless type, and what Harold Wolff defined as the angry nonparticipant. Like a general who has led his men to defeat and now has trouble getting them to obey orders, his ego falters in its control. And his aggression, since it has failed as a constructive tool, becomes destructive, and turns into hostility.

Dependency and constructive aggression know how to work together; dependency and hostility only get in each other's way. For instance, Warren is dependent on his boss for that thirty thousand dollars a year. But he wishes his boss dead because it isn't thirty-five thousand. Were his wish to come true, however, he wouldn't even get the thirty thousand.

When hostility and dependency churn together, anxiety results. And the anxiety then proceeds to increase the hostility: Warren blames his employer for his anxious state. At the same time his hostility makes him feel guilty—so much so that to make up for it he may indeed start playing a servile role, the way Sevringhaus does. Or he may turn the hostility inward against himself and become depressed. That way he can expend the hostility, and at the same time assuage the guilt by punishing himself. Depression has a way of bringing the emotional economy together—which may account for its popularity—but it's not much of a life.

Simplest of all, of course, Warren can bury the whole mess—hostility, anxiety, guilt, and all—and go on as if nothing is wrong. But this doesn't solve the salary problem, and it doesn't solve the emotional problem either. The emotions, buried, are buried alive. They may be out of sight, but in consequence they're out of control, shut off from the rational and integrating dominion of the ego.

CHAPTER 6

How the Body Handles Stress

Lying cheerily in a hospital bed after a hip operation some years back, Hans Selye observed: "You know, we are still evolving from the Neanderthal mold; the trouble is, our problems evolve quickly, but our bodies evolve slowly, very slowly. People like to assume that the body always works intelligently. But this is not so. The body is like the mind. It, too, gets confused and makes mistakes."

Where stress is concerned, what usually happens is that mind and body make the same mistake together, through physiological actions and reactions that unbalance the delicate relationships among molecules, cells, tissues, organs, and systems of the body—one adjustment demanding another, and the other yet another, and so on. The neuro-endocrine system plays a leading role in this process, and when the stress is emotional in nature, it is the brain that sets the process off.

Comparing the mind with the brain is a little like comparing a poem to a mountain, though less so than it used to be; and perhaps one day we will be able to close the gap—to describe, for instance, exactly what physical events occur in the central nervous system when guilt is felt. When this happens, if it ever does, the two fields of psychology and neurology will become one.

But even today we know enough to make some correlations. Rational processes such as memory, planning, perception and intellectual rumination—in short, many of the everyday functions of the ego—take place, we know, in the cerebral cortex of the brain. And many of the instinctive drives—hunger, sex, sleep, pleasure, to name a few—seem to be activated in the hypothalamic area; at any rate they can be stimulated or inhibited by electrical manipulation of that area. So can fight and flight impulses.

To put it rather simply, the hypothalamus is a kind of first sergeant, passing on orders from the brain to the rest of the body and seeing to it that they are carried out. It can do this because within it are gathered the neural connections of the autonomic nervous system, which regulates all the involuntary organs of the body—liver, heart, kidneys and so forth. And the hypothalamus also controls the endocrine system, because it activates the pituitary gland, which in turn activates most of the other endocrine glands.

The whole arrangement is deeply complicated, but the basic principles that underlie it can be stated fairly simply.

One of these is the principle of balance. Any animal must react to threats if it is to survive, but at the same time it must not overreact. An antelope is wise to run from a lion, but not if it runs so fast and so far that its heart bursts. To prevent this kind of thing the living organism contains many safeguards, some of them physical, some emotional. For example, there are few threats that evoke either pure fear or pure anger, perhaps there are none; the two emotions mix together and balance each other, rendering people's behavior more realistic. Without the cautionary influence of fear, anger becomes explosive and self-damaging. Pure fear, unalloyed by the assertive quality of anger, degenerates into helplessness.

Like the emotions, the neuro-endocrine system, too, is full of checks and balances. The cerebral cortex and the hypothalamus operate together in this fashion. And so do the endocrine hormones.

One part of the adrenal gland, for instance, the adrenal cortex, secretes a group of hormones known as corticoids. Some of these are what Selye called proinflammatory, and some are anti-inflammatory. In situations of mild stress it is the pro-inflammatory corticoids that dominate, and it is easy to see why. As we learned earlier, inflammation is a very effective way to handle a particular kind of stress situation—the entrance of a foreign object, such as a splinter or microbe, into the body. When this happens, inflammation walls the invader off in one area and goes to work to destroy it there, leaving the rest of the body free to operate normally.

Nevertheless, there are many situations where inflammation is damaging. In a vital organ like the liver or the heart, it can cause serious trouble. And if it fails, as it sometimes does, to confine the threat—if a microbe escapes and attacks the rest of the body—then inflammation ceases to be useful. It is for these reasons that the adrenal glands secrete the anti-inflammatory corticoids as well as the pro-inflammatory ones; and when stress is severe, prolonged, and general throughout the body, then the AC's predominate over the PC's. Cortisone is one of the anti-inflammatory corticoids. In 1944 it was synthesized as a drug, and today is used by patients with such diverse ailments as arthritis and poison ivy to reduce their inflammatory aches and itches.

Still a third kind of balance in the neuro-endocrine system takes place through a simple process with a fancy name: negative feedback. Negative feedback is in constant operation throughout the body. What if Warren gave way to his hypothalamic impulses, for instance, and attacked his employer? When Warren's right arm commenced to swing, his sensory nerves would keep him advised every millimeter of the way: "No, no, too high . . . That's better, but a shade lower

. . . No, too low, too low! *Now* you've got it! Right on the button!'' At the same time, his pituitary would not only be sending all kinds of hormones into his blood, but would also be assessing the results by measuring the chemical content of the blood returning to it, and making adjustments as needed.

The neuro-endocrine system is not only a balanced system. It is a varied system. We respond to stress both in an overall way, by means of hormones which pass to every part of the body, and in a selective way, by the action of specific nerves on specific muscles. We can also respond briefly, or at length. If Warren hits his boss, adrenaline will help him do it effectively, and so will the motor and sensory nerves of his right arm. The whole business only takes a moment. But when it comes to dealing with the consequences of his act, which may persist for months, he will need the longer-term stress hormones, the corticoids and thyroxine.

Beyond these general principles, just how does the neuro-endocrine system, our physical machinery for handling stress, operate? It is a little like the old song:

> The hip bone's connected to the thigh bone.
> And the thigh bone's connected to the knee bone.
> And the knee bone's connected to the shin bone.

But instead of thigh bone and shin bone you must use such terms as the splanchnic nerve and deoxycorticosterone, which is harder. However, let us try to reason together.

We will start with the *hypothalamus*, a part of the brain which, as we have seen, has a shifting and somewhat troubled relationship with that higher portion of the brain called the *cerebral cortex:* the cerebral cortex does its best to keep the hypothalamus under control, with but mixed results. The hypothalamus, as we have also seen, controls the *autonomic nervous system,* which in turn helps control the internal organs of the body. And we have seen that the hypothalamus also controls the so-called master gland of the endocrine system, the *pituitary*.

This pituitary master gland consists of two lobes. One, the *posterior lobe,* is made mainly of nervous tissue which, when stimulated, releases into the blood a hormone known as *vasopressin*. Vasopressin contracts the muscles in the walls of the arteries, raising the blood pressure.

The *anterior lobe* of the pituitary, by contrast, contains mostly glandular, rather than nerve, tissue, and of its six major hormones only two are activated by stress.* The first is *ACTH* (AdrenoCorticoTrophic Hormone). The second is the *thyrotrophic hormone,* or TTH. Both of these have powerful effects on the body, but only indirectly: what they do is to stimulate two other glands—TTH, the thyroid gland; and ACTH, the adrenal cortex. The adrenal cortex in turn helps to stimulate the pancreas, so that in the end the pituitary affects almost all the endocrine glands.

It is important to note that the pituitary doesn't just pour forth a little of everything when stimulated; it is selective in its secretions. This is because the message-carrying substances from the hypothalamus are themselves selective, and indeed, though their chemistry is as yet undiscovered, have been given truly Baroque names, such as the Corticotrophin Releasing Factor, the Gonadotrophin Releasing Factor, and the Thyrotrophin Releasing Factor. In such fashion is the hip bone connected to the thigh bone and on down the line. Even ACTH and TTH, though both are stimulated by stress, don't as a rule increase together. The

---

*Of the rest, three are sex hormones and one is somatotrophin, the hormone regulating body growth. The supply of these hormones actually decreases as the stress hormones increase, which is why stress can reduce sexual drive, or stunt a child's growth.

first cold day of autumn causes a rise in TTH because thyroxine, the thyroid hormone, makes people warmer by raising their metabolic rate—which is why you feel peppy in winter and lazy in summer. But temperature has little effect on ACTH.

In fact, the relative behavior of the thyroid and the adrenal cortex shows some of that balancing tendency so common in the neuro-endocrine system. People with busy thyroids are likely to have a quiet adrenal cortex, and vice versa.

The *thyroid* gland is located in the throat, adjacent to the larynx or voice box, and a few inches below the pituitary. Its secretions set the body's basal metabolism—which is the rate at which the individual cells burn oxygen—and help determine how much energy a person has. If the metabolism is very slow, the person tires easily, feels cold, and is probably overweight; much of the food he eats is not burned off so it has to go into storage. Conversely, if the metabolic rate is too high, the person may be excessively thin, sweat readily, and feel nervous and shaky. His heart beats too fast, and his breathing is unusually deep and rapid. Like the person with the underactive thyroid, however, he too feels tired much of the time, for even when he sleeps his body is overworking. Both types may go on to develop a goiter—a swelling in the throat caused by enlargement of the thyroid gland.

Thyroxine, the chief thyroid hormone, not only affects the speed at which the body consumes fuel, it is also important in the maturing process—including physical growth, but particularly sexual and mental development. Unless they are treated, young children whose thyroids are severely underactive become cretins: dwarfs in size, who never experience puberty and are mentally retarded. Interestingly, Franz Alexander writes that many people with *over*active thyroids share a common emotional problem and it may help to cause their physical condition. The problem is dependency—

the feeling that they can't cope with life without a mother's help. When this help is unavailable, they swing to the opposite extreme—feigning a maturity they do not really possess, and driving themselves to take on more and more responsibility, particularly if it involves the care of dependent people such as children or invalids. For unknown reasons the majority of hyperthyroid patients are women.

Probably the most complicated of the endocrine glands are the *adrenals,* which lie on top of the two kidneys. Like the pituitary, the adrenal glands have two sections, and again, like the pituitary, one of the sections consists mainly of nervous tissue and the other mainly of glandular tissue. The neural section, because it is the interior section, is called the *adrenal medulla* (medulla means inner substance), and appropriately it is stimulated not by a hormone but by a nerve, known as the splanchnic nerve. The hormones that the adrenal medulla secretes are *adrenaline* and *nor adrenaline.*

Everyone knows what adrenaline feels like—it is the sensation you get after a bus almost runs you down, or a bolt of lightning strikes the tree outside your window: a sudden burst of rather marvelously bodily exhilaration that would probably be thoroughly pleasant if it were not so closely associated with fear. In fact, some endocrinologists suspect that adrenaline is a fear hormone, and that nor adrenaline is an anger hormone. But as fear usually contains some anger, and anger some fear, so adrenaline and nor adrenaline are commonly released together into the blood in varying proportions. Adrenaline runs higher in rabbits and older children, nor adrenaline higher in lions and babies (presumably because babies are as yet too ignorant to feel much fear).

What do adrenaline and nor adrenaline do to you, besides making you feel that rather eerie exuberance?

They equip you for emergency action—first through their effects on the cardiovascular system. They constrict your arteries and make your heart beat faster, in order to rush more blood to your muscles and brain. They draw the blood back from the skin and also quicken its clotting time, so you will bleed less if injured. And to fight possible infection, they raise your white blood count.

Second, they take action to speed up your metabolism. They increase your red blood count, delivering more oxygen to the cells so you burn your fuel faster; and they increase the supply of fuel itself, by stimulating the liver and the muscles to release sugar into the blood. When this happens the pancreas measures the rise in blood sugar, and begins pouring insulin into the blood, enabling the excess sugar to enter the cells.

Adrenaline performs one other important function in relation to stress: it cooperates with thyroxine, the hormone of the thyroid. When thyroxine measures high in the blood, all the body tissues seem to become more sensitive to adrenaline. Generally speaking, thyroxine is a long-term measure for dealing with stress, and adrenaline is short term. Thyroxine fights wars, adrenaline fights battles. But just as wars consist of a sequence of battles, so thyroxine and adrenaline are needed together in most stress situations.

Surrounding the adrenal medulla, where adrenaline and noradrenaline are manufactured, is the exterior covering of glandular tissue known as the *adrenal cortex* (cortex means outer part). This is the area of the adrenals that is activated by ACTH, the hormone from the pituitary, and it is here that the so-called proinflammatory and anti-inflammatory corticoids are produced. There are over thirty of these adrenal corticoids, so there is little point in identifying them all, but they do break into two groups, generally called the mineralocorticoids and the glucocorticoids. The mineralocorticoids are the ones that promote inflammation.

Primarily, however, the ACTH ups the level of the glucocorticoids, and these are anti-inflammatory in action. Interestingly, ACTH also tends to reduce cholesterol in the body—in fact there is reason to believe that one function of the adrenal cortex is to control cholesterol levels, possibly even manufacturing its own hormones out of cholesterol itself.

Of the body's endocrine glands, then, five—the pituitary, the thyroid, the adrenal medulla, the adrenal cortex, and the pancreas—play complex and important roles in our reactions to stress. What about the sexual glands?

The sexual glands—the testes in males, and the ovaries and placenta in females—would seem irrelevant: in fact a rise in stress hormones actually causes a fall in sex hormones. But even here the situation is not so simple. Without going into the complicated structure and functions of these glands, it is important to realize that the hormones they secrete, particularly the male androgens, have a substantial influence on aggressive feelings. Aggressiveness is one of the emotions people use in dealing with stressful situations. But if it is excessive, aggression can also cause stress, disturbing one's emotional economy, as well as one's relations with the rest of the world. As such, it can go on to activate the whole neuro-endocrine stress machinery.

When the wonderfully precise neuro-endocrine system becomes imprecise, there is trouble. Repair is difficult and replacement at present pretty much out of the question: endocrine transplants have been attempted in humans but are still highly experimental. And while medical treatment with ACTH drugs sometimes revive overworked adrenals, the same is not true of all the hormones. Insulin injections, though they keep a diabetic patient alive and functioning fairly normally, do not restore the pancreas. As for the nervous system, it cannot regenerate like most of the other tissues of the body. An area of brain cells killed by injury or lack of blood is dead forever.

What makes a neuro-endocrine system go wrong? Sometimes it is a matter of what you're born with. As in buying a car, you can come up with a lemon, and heredity is a common factor in such ailments as hyperthyroidism and diabetes. Sometimes life itself is the problem—some people are beset from early childhood by one insoluble problem after another, until their stress equipment gradually wears down from overwork.

Still other people come up against a normal quota of problems, but react to them in an unbalanced fashion, perhaps overutilizing the thyroid, for example.

This kind of highly localized response to stress at first glance looks sensible—in fact it closely resembles the mechanism of inflammation which we talked about a few pages back. Behind both lies the principle of specialization: spare the whole by delegating to the part. But it only works when it works, so to speak—when it actually solves the specific stress problem. If the response is wrong, then the problem persists; and then the response persists too, if it's the only one you have learned how to make. Adrenaline alone is not going to raise Warren's salary, just his blood pressure, and eventually his body may develop serious hypertension as a result. Many people are suffering from chronic illnesses today because they possess excessively specialized coping mechanisms that are not really capable of coping.

CHAPTER 7

How the Mind Betrays the Body

The whole lesson of Warren's childhood was that if he worked hard and was a good boy, he might go anywhere. Now he knows otherwise. But what is he to do? It is too late to change character: he's still a good boy who works hard, but a defeated and angry one now.

Nevertheless, emotion does out, one way or another. We have got to say what we feel and mean; when we can't say it in words or actions, we say it physiologically. A simple illustration of this basic principle is the lie detector test: truth, denied in words, literally emerges through the skin.*

In the twentieth century we spend a good deal of time denying the truth about our feelings, perhaps because our means for expressing these feelings have become quite meager. We seldom allow ourselves to take physical action—both *fight* and *flight,* the standard animal responses, are frowned upon. And we have lost most of the so-called projective techniques that primitive societies developed to explain and to solve human difficulties.

Eric D. Wittkower recalls that in Ghana, for in-

---

*R. D. Laing, in *The Divided Self,* recalls the story of a schizophrenic patient who, during the course of a lie detector test, was asked if he was really Napoleon. The patient responded no—but the equipment demonstrated he was lying.

stance, a man suffering from impotence consulted a native healer, and received the following treatment:

> The healer divined the patient and came to the conclusion that the patient's impotence was due to his sister who was a witch. The sister was called in; she admitted that she was a witch and that she had stolen her brother's testicles. She had buried them in an ant heap. "But then the ants will have eaten up your brother's testicles," the healer said. "No," the sister replied, "they can't have done this because I put them into a tin box." They all went to the ant heap, took out the tin box, which of course was empty, and returned the testicles to the rightful owner who lived happily ever after.*

Our approach may be more rational, but does it work as well? We blame our problems on ourselves, not on witches, and seek to solve them not through charms and incantations but through inner change, a very difficult procedure. When this is not effective, we dispose of the problem by burying it—or think that we do.

People like Warren don't choose the psychosomatic response. It chooses them, because they are not in a position to make any other choice and their feelings must find release somewhere.

Then why does stress disease happen the *way* it happens? Why does one patient come down with ulcers, another with a heart attack, and a third with a skin allergy?

First, the psychosomatic response varies from individual to individual because everyone's physical equipment varies: the defective part of the engine fails first. Sometimes problems are inherited, such as a

*From *Modern Perspectives in World Psychiatry*, edited by John G. Howells, Brunner-Mazel, Inc., 1971.

pancreatic deficiency in diabetes. But sometimes they are acquired, through misuse of originally healthy bodily equipment over a period of many years. This is true of some people with chronic respiratory diseases. Perhaps in the first few years of life a little boy comes for one reason or another to fear aggression, in himself and others; he learns to avoid sports and physical exertion of all kinds; he is soft spoken, does not scream and shout like his brothers and sisters, seldom even cries. His grandparents may approve these qualities in him, but his lungs will suffer, simply because he does not use them enough. He may also form an unconscious habit when under strain of suspending his breath slightly. Most children do this when they are attempting a difficult manual task, such as building a house of cards, or learning to write in script. It is a natural expression of the need for care, for restrained control. But some children feel this need in any situation of pressure. Under stress they can never really let themselves go. They take a deep breath—but they let out only a shallow one.

Such a child is using a harmful pattern of breathing in order to repress his feelings, and when he gets older he is very likely to carry the process further by becoming a smoker. Still later in life he may develop chronic bronchitis or emphysema. Significantly, the real problem in emphysema is expiration. You've got to get the bad air out before the good air can enter. An emphysema patient's lungs are always partially inflated, laden with carbon dioxide and other irritating wastes that the diseased lungs cannot get rid of.

The psychosomatic response also varies because personalities vary: the average coronary patient is very different from the average colitis patient, as we saw in Part Two. Beyond physical and personality differences, however, people vary in their illnesses because they attach different meanings to these illnesses. Sometimes this happens by accident. A kidney ailment may coincide with an episode of challenge or loss in a person's life, and thereafter challenge or loss may evoke kidney symptoms by simple association. But more often the meaning of an illness is something people learn, and they are very apt to learn it from their parents. A girl whose mother gets high blood pressure when angry learns that anger is a function of the arteries. In other words, an organ or system of the body can become a metaphor in the life of the individual, and she will employ it whenever she feels threatened. If her life is placid and easy, the trigger may never be pulled. But if it is stormy and full of difficulties, she will react in the way she has been taught to react.

Stewart Wolf called such physiological behavior the "as if" response, and characterized a number of diseases accordingly. Thus, patients with hypertension are behaving as if they were about to lose blood in combat. Ulcer patients behave as if they were continually about to devour (not only that, but, in Dr. Wolf's speculation, to devour the body of some adversary, whom they unconsciously wish to kill and eat). Patients with coronary artery disease behave as if great effort were forever demanded of them. And the diabetic acts starved.

Once rooted, the psychosomatic response gradually becomes a habit—and a very hard one to break. By comparison, giving up smoking is easy because will power is on your side: you *can* make up your mind to stop buying cigarettes, and to refuse any that are offered to you, and though the effort may cause you ghastly anguish, if you are strong-minded and sufficiently motivated you will learn to live without tobacco. But your glands and your autonomic nervous system are something else again.* Besides, if you live

*Actually, in recent years it has been discovered that some people *can*

with an illness long enough you gradually discover that it does things for you.

You learn that sickness is a very good way to get taken care of—and the sicker you are, the truer this is. The patient with mild arthritis still must earn a living and fulfill obligations, although the stiffness and pain actually add to the difficulties of daily life. But let your condition become severe and all that changes. You are hospitalized, perhaps operated on. Others must take over your responsibilities as best they can. Even the pain has a tricky way of serving you, because it eases your conscience. It is your way of saying, "This may look like a bed of roses, just lying here being nursed, but don't be fooled: I really hurt."

Pain also gives you the right to take analgesics and other drugs, for which some people develop an affinity powerful enough to outlive their physical symptoms. At the Wilhelmina Hospital in Amsterdam, group psychotherapy greatly improved the breathing problems of asthma patients, but it did not change their reliance on cortisone sprays and the like. They would resort to these medications even when they felt well—"just in case," or "to be on the safe side," as they explained.

This simple longing to be taken care of is only one of the feelings people express by getting sick. Another is guilt, which calls out for painful, self-punishing afflictions like arthritis and migraine. A third—and the most important of all, probably—is the feeling of anger. Karen Horney, the psychoanalyst, suggested that the biggest disturbing force in most people's lives is no longer the repressed sexuality of Freud's Vienna, but simple repressed hostility, and there is much to support her contention. Certainly few doctors today come up against the kind of patient Freud made famous: the upper-middle-class lady with hysterical

---

deliberately lower their own blood pressure, or reduce their gastric secretions, if they are trained to do so (see p. 188).

symptoms—paralysis or blindness—that could be cured by uncovering her hidden sexual longings. Instead they deal with coronary and hypertension cases, with arthritics, with the accident-prone—people whose illnesses appear to have a very real connection with unacknowledged combativeness.

In the previous chapter we learned how anger can start up the whole neuro-endocrine machine for aggressive physical action and keep it running, eventually wearing out vulnerable body parts if action never occurs. This is one of the paths anger follows in stress disease. Another is simple muscular tension. Muscular tension can take benign forms, such as nail biting, or general restlessness. It can also cause backache and headaches. But in a severely repressed person, even these expressions are inhibited. Such a person forces himself to keep calm on the outside, but may be in all kinds of trouble within, for his tension then passes to the autonomic nervous system, where it can cause spasms in the digestive tract or lungs, or in the muscles of the artery walls. Flanders Dunbar treated many high-blood-pressure cases with psychotherapy, and she observed that as patients began to get better their previous composure was usually replaced by a great deal of physical restlessness which disappeared when they recovered.

One of the sadder stories in medical literature comes from Dr. Dunbar again, the case of a young woman with a club foot, a deformity certainly not psychosomatic in origin, but psychosomatic in function: although she was born with the club foot, she had used it all her life to explain away anything that went wrong. For instance, she had wanted to be a teacher, but gave up teacher training because she felt the children stared at her foot; and she insisted all her problems could be solved by surgery.

Finally the foot was operated on—only to be fractured in a fall as soon as she got on crutches; and after she recovered she soon fell and broke her other leg—"an expression," in Dr. Dundar's words, "of the patient's unconscious need to keep the deformed extremity as a defense against and cover for her more fundamental personality conflicts." Dr. Dunbar added, "With her recovery, she became increasingly schizophrenic. On discharge psychotherapy was recommended but proved not to be feasible because the patient left town. She returned a year later, the foot and leg in perfect condition but . . . a full-blown psychotic . . ."

The files of medicine are full of such examples. Harold Wolff describes the great inner serenity in a patient with advanced ulcerative colitis. Dr. Samuel Silverman tells of a patient with chronic depression which lifts whenever he suffers an ulcer attack. Psychotics suffer less physical disease than the general population. And people in wartime are physically healthier than they are in peacetime—seemingly because war provides an acceptable outlet for hostility feelings. During the Six Day War in Israel in 1967, the death rate from disease fell even in homes for the aged. And when Germany invaded Holland in 1940, Dutch doctors were astonished by the overnight recovery of many patients, some of them seriously ill in hospital beds, whose symptoms evaporated when the Germans came.

Some doctors warn against the dangers of "curing" certain patients of the physical symptoms they have come to depend on. Unless this kind of patient receives counseling or unless his life changes for the better, he frequently suffers a recurrence of the old symptoms, or else acquires new ones, or runs into emotional problems. Dr. Silverman did a follow-up in his hospital on thirty ulcer cases corrected by surgical gastrectomy. Of these, seventeen suffered recurrent ulcers. four of them severe; four developed hypertension; five developed asthma; one came down with tuberculosis, and seventeen showed other bodily symptoms of anxiety.

Such patients have reached the point where they can no longer get along without their afflictions, which in the words of Dr. Wolff, "afford relative tranquility and in many instances, a workable and useful life adjustment, becoming a nuisance or menace only when they threaten the goal of survival."

Many stress diseases can and do kill; and certainly most people fear death. But, paradoxically, these two facts may work together to increase the actual amount of illness in the world. Starting with Freud, who observed the phenomenon on a child's play, psychologists have called attention to what is known as the repetition compulsion—the need to reenact major personal problems in the small and large occasions of daily living. In the words of Erik Erikson, "The individual unconsciously arranges for variations of an original theme which he has not learned either to overcome or to live with; he tries to master a situation which in its original form had been too much for him by meeting it repeatedly and of his own accord."*

An original theme which he has not learned either to overcome or to live with: isn't this almost a definition of the power death has in most people's lives? And is sickness, at least in part, an attempt to pose the problem of death and then, by recovering, to seem to solve it?

Anxiety about death, plus a longing to be taken care of: these make a powerful combination. Where are you free to indulge both your deepest fears and your deepest longings? In bed, sick, may be the answer. True, you may hurt, you may feel terrible, you may be afraid. But everyone loves you. You are brought flowers and warm soup. You are encouraged to sleep

*Erik Erikson, *Childhood and Society.* W. W. Norton and Company, 1950.

as much as possible. Otherwise little is expected of you. You spend the days catching up on your almost forgotten fantasy life while your doctor shoulders the responsibility of bringing about your recovery.

Your doctor bears the responsibility, but you get the credit—for doesn't everyone congratulate you when you are better? And you congratulate yourself. You have come once more through the valley of the shadow; you have confronted death and beaten it again.

Even when its effects are mild, the psychosomatic response has drawbacks. It not only damages bodies, it damages lives. It is a strategy aimed at protecting people, but it ends up dehumanizing them in many ways. We consist of our weaknesses, along with our strengths; and we have to be able to exercise both. Tuning out one or two aspects of our nature results in a tuning down of the whole—a lowering of spontaneity, of vitality, of humanness. People who cannot feel and express anger are often people who cannot feel and express love.

Then again, although psychosomatic illness may first crop up in your life as a response to some problem you have no other way of dealing with, as the years pass it tends to crop up again, and yet again, and increasingly in situations that are not really all that difficult—in response to problems you *could* solve, but by now you're so used to responding physiologically that it has become your way of life. Something can be said for physical symptoms that help you through an impossible situation. If the situation could be changed, however, but your symptoms excuse you from taking action, then you are in the grip of a truly damaging habit.

That habit can set in very early. An eight-year-old who is having trouble in school may come down with recurrent stomach upsets. Adolescent acne often occurs in a setting of hostility, strong sexual drive, and guilt. Even colds and flu can be connected with emotional problems, as we saw in Part Two. But these are minor ailments which, considering the services they may render, are at least conceivably worth the price they exact. In many people this balance tends to change—and the price to go up—with the onset of middle age. The body at this point begins showing signs of wear in general—particularly those parts of the body that are used to express feelings and problems. The eight-year-old with the stomach upset becomes the forty-year-old with colitis or ulcers. Moreover, what was originally only a vague tendency has in the course of thirty years of use developed into an automatic reaction, one on which the person increasingly relies as the problems accumulate and the capacity for handling them commences to decline. You begin to see that for all your efforts, you are really going to die in the end anyway, and besides you are by now rather tired of making these efforts, and the possibility of someone else taking the load seems only fair.

All these elements—biological, behavioral, and emotional—come together at about the same time; then along comes one more very human complication, rooted in the past, which may be what finally tips the balance toward serious chronic disease.

In order for children to grow into adults, they must break away from their dependency on their parents. This is not easy. They have grown accustomed to the comforts of being taken care of and told what to do, and even their parents do not always welcome the change. But change they must, and so about the time of adolescence they set about it, chiefly by summoning up latent forces of hostility and turning them against their parents, and against the older generation generally, as part of the renunciation process. And the harder the struggle, the more hostile the renunciation, until teenagers may find themselves in violent opposition to everything their parents stand for, from their politics to the way they smile to the kind of food they eat.

This behavior carries over from adolescence well into adult life, as people work to define themselves as independent adults by establishing their place in the world and founding families. Even when the worst is over and the crisis past, traces of basic hostility may persist for many years, for a part of them continues to wish they were little children again, with nothing to accomplish and no decisions to make.

But the situation finally does change—chiefly because the possibilities for depending themselves change. By the time you reach your middle forties your parents are usually into their seventies and in no position to take care of you—often it's you who must take care of them. In any case, they no longer constitute a threat to independence.

Besides, the years of hostility have bred an accumulation of guilt, which, as the threat subsides, now comes to bear in your behavior. A spirit of atonement takes up residence within you. Old verities turn up in your speech. Your politics grow more conservative. You may start going to church again. Your values alter and kindness may become a more important virtue to you than determination, reality more to the point than ideals. You have the sense of relaxing and at last seeing and accepting the truth about life.

Freud called this deferred obedience, and it crops up not only in beliefs and attitudes. At fifty, you may suddenly develop a vague craving for tapioca pudding, or find yourself habitually cracking your knuckles, irritating your spouse by the habit just as your father used to irritate your mother. You may also start suffering from shortness of breath and occasional chest pains, and not feel too surprised—after all, it was a heart attack that killed your father.

PART FOUR

What You Can Do About It— Personal Solutions for the Stress Problem

So it is stress of a peculiarly subjective sort that is the principal marauder in our society: not the pressure of a gun against the ribs, but a nagging worry about being mugged; not outright competition from a rival stalking the same forest for game, but a cutting memo circulating in a quiet office organization; not the dreaded appearance of diphtheria symptoms in a member of the family, but the uneasy feeling that one's child is out in the city courting unhappiness and destruction. Our instinctive body responses are of little use against problems such as these. Nevertheless, we go right on responding, with the result that we not only stew in the problems—we stew in the responses too. Can these responses be changed?

In the very long run they change of themselves— which is why people today are taller, smarter and more dexterous than their prehistoric ancestors. This is the story of evolution. Faced with the stress of a new challenge, the species learns to adapt by altering its physical equipment. But it is a slow process, much too slow to help the individual person.

So the individual tries other means. In very early times he tried magic. Special amulets, formal hunting rituals, rain dances, and witch doctors—these were irrational practices, but many of them actually worked, simply by inducing a state of trust and confidence in their practitioners. Then came religion, and for centuries man called his mind his soul. "Religion is not psychotherapy [but] it functioned as such for two millenia in the western world," wrote Dr. Walter Bromberg in his definitive study, The Mind of Man.

In the present century religion as a therapeutic force has yielded visibly and steadily to science. Yet faith itself continues to play a powerful role. "In God we trust" has become "In science we trust," but what really matters is that we go on trusting. The subjective is as important as ever.

The concluding section of this book is an exploration of the techniques of science—both laboratory and folk science—into which people today are putting faith and effort—and money—in attempts to quell their nebulous anxieties, as well as the specific bodily aches that so often accompany them. The simplest of these techniques is physical conditioning: exercise and diet. The most complicated is psychotherapy, a multibillion-dollar annual business in the United States. A third is pharmacology, the source of all the countless pills and potions that overflow our medicine cabinets, and in particular of the mood-altering drugs which have changed some people's lives simply by making them feel pleasant and often a little sleepy.

But the pressures of twentieth-century stress are severe, and if the clergyman has not always proved adequate to handle them, neither has the family doctor, nor the gym coach, nor the druggist, nor the psychotherapist, not entirely. For additional help Americans are now turning to space age electronics, in the form of biological-feedback machines; and to ancient Vedic rituals like Yoga (with modern marketing applied to them). They are also turning to one another, by en-

rolling in support groups, based on the idea that ordinary people can help other ordinary people break through the pressures and find serenity, meaning and wholeness.

CHAPTER 8

Altering Your Equipment: Exercise and Diet

Twenty centuries ago, when Hannibal first used elephants in his military campaigns, some citizen probably said, "Now, with these new weapons, warfare has become too terrible; there can be no more wars." In the centuries since Hannibal, the same reaction to an excessive arms technology has been voiced again and again—and with very much the same effect, or lack of it. Our own peace-loving democracy has spent more than a quarter of the present century at some form of warfare, and we annually expend a huge proportion of our national wealth on weapons that make elephants seem very amusing creatures indeed.

Hostile aggressiveness is not only a collective national trait, it is a personal one too, and lies deep within all of us. It powers not only our careers, but also our games, such as football, and our drama; even our comedies often have a sadistic edge. Look at the violent way we operate automobiles. We seem in a sense always to be threatening personal war.

Turning off violent instincts altogether is probably not possible, nor, as we have seen, is it necessarily wise to try. People were born to fight, and when they don't permit themselves to fight others, they usually end up fighting themselves. What we need are ways of fighting that do not injure and kill—but otherwise, the more physical, the better. Long before Hannibal's time sports and exercise were invented to fill this need, and they are increasingly important in the twentieth century, as the kind of work people do involves less and less physical exertion. One of the many stresses we suffer from is the stress of our own pent-up aggressive drives. When we express these drives in physical action, we are better off.

But exercise is useful in another way, too. It not only dispels one form of stress in our lives, it also enables us to bear up better against stress in general. An engineering analogy comes to mind. Structural engineers in the past fifty years have learned, before assembling buildings and bridges, to *pre*-stress parts of them by applying preliminary loadings against the eventual anticipated loads that will come when the structures are completed and in use. Conditioning the body can accomplish the same kind of thing. A person who is in good physical condition will withstand the assault of a virus, or a spell of overwork—or even a quarrel with the foreman—better than someone who isn't.

Health aside, being in good physical shape is, of course, quite simply very pleasant—indeed, somewhat blissful. A deep receptive peace comes with being tired after having used one's body hard and well. Like post-coital relaxation, it is close to complete physical repose.

The very opposite of this state is much more common in everyday life in our country, from what doctors in general practice tell us. One of the complaints they hear most often is of exhaustion without exertion, a chronic tiredness seeping in on their patients in much the same way depression does. Like depression, it can become a way of life. Although the sufferer complains of his tiredness, at the same time he may defend it with surprising, if sluggish, ferocity. It justifies everything—his troubles at the office, his dwindling sex life, his inability to control his children. And in his condition, he can't work up much interest in how his body looks or feels.

Nevertheless, he goes to see his physician: maybe some unusual malady will be discovered. But none is. Instead, the doctor recommends an exercise class. The patient only nods. His eye is on the prescription pad: *Why not a pill?* he is thinking. The doctor observes his glance and ignores it. "Arrange to join a group," he exhorts the patient. "Play some tennis. Bicycle. Or take long walks: walk to work. You won't be so tired so much of the time."

And the patient puts on his shirt and goes home feeling worse than ever. Exercise! How can he exercise when he's already too tired to get through the day?

There are many factors that militate against the beginning of any regimen of physical conditioning. On the face of it it seems faintly ridiculous to deliberately work up a sweat in an air-conditioned world. There's something masochistic about it. Besides, there is the problem of finding a reasonably priced place and a time to do the damned exercises. Perhaps the biggest deterrent is the suspicion that it is all ritualistic folklore that will not do you any good anyway.

Also an air of charlatanism clings to the whole idea of conditioning. Series of fads and fetishes have swept the country, from exercise wheels, to the gruelling Royal Canadian Air Force routine, back to the great psychological sells of the Adonis-makers, such as Charles Atlas. In the backs of thousands of closets lie unused barbells. A bedroom exercise bike probably has a higher markdown in price, proportionately, than a used car because so many of the bikes are back on the market after a season or two. The exercise masters of the past have been more interested in merchandising than in real conditioning.

This is no longer true, however. In recent years conditioning has become less of an occasional craze, and more of a crusade. Part of this change can be traced back to the late President John F. Kennedy, a youngish man who knew both the joys of fitness and, then, considerable physical suffering. He set up the President's Council on Physical Fitness, and conditioning began to be taken more seriously. Careers in research started opening up, to be filled by some very competent scientists. Privately operated gymnasiums have opened all over the country.

In 1965, the National Aeronautics and Space Administration in Washington set up an exercise program that put special emphasis on the detection of potential heart problems and the reinforcement of physical abilities to resist them. All NASA employees above a certain rank, and all employees over forty years old—a total of about two thousand—were given annual physicals, including the usual electrocardiogram (EKG). There was also a very unusual EKG, which began at 8:00 A.M. on a normal working day and continued all day. Individuals were wired up with portable EKG devices and wore them under their shirts as they went about their work. Besides following their regular patterns of activity, they were asked to perform certain additional tasks, such as walking up and down several flights of stairs. The EKG recorded the results on a very slow tape, and at the end of the day the supervising physician sat with the patient, ran the tape off on a fast spool, and asked a few questions.

Some interesting variables were found concerning what produces stress in different individuals. Climbing three flights of stairs raises one woman's pulse rate to 120 beats a minute, but an argument with her secretary sends it up to 160. One man's pulse rate peaks when he has to attend an office conference.

Each person examined got recommendations, if needed, on both diet and exercise, and many were advised to work out three times a week in the NASA "stress laboratory." This was a gymnasium equipped with numerous control devices which helped users stay within their individual maximum safe effort. Four cardiovascular-stress exercises—running on a treadmill, pedaling a stationary bicycle, pulling on a rowing machine, and most strenuous of all, jumping rope—were carefully spaced out by milder muscletoning routines using barbells and medicine balls. The pulse rate engendered by a particular task dropped as people acquired proficiency.

Special attention was paid to those labeled "cardiac susceptible." EKG tapes indicated that carefully controlled exercise actually improved a number of suspicious heart rhythms.

Another conditioning expert is Dr. Kenneth H. Cooper, who, during his early years as an Air Force medical officer, came up with an interesting theory concerning the benefits of regular exercise. He called it *aerobics,* has published a number of medical papers and several popular books on the subject, and, now a civilian, gives it his full time.

What virtually all these professionals in the conditioning field insist, with persuasive cogency, is that the only exercise which really improves the body is a carefully programmed approach to exhaustion. They have nothing against the old bend-and-stretch rituals. They will accept a certain amount of weight lifting, although most of them regard isometrics as useless to health. Pushups and situps they recommend as tonic for certain muscle groups. But what these doctors prescribe most enthusiastically are running, jumping rope, long brisk walks (preferably three miles or more in an hour), swimming, bicycling, and such active sports as strenuous rowing, handball, squash and basketball. These are what they call the endurance activities, and these, they maintain, will fortify the body against stress. Dr. Cooper's aerobics theory, basically, is that the better condition people are in, the more oxygen they are actually able to use out of the air that they inhale. They may not need this extra oxygen most of the time, but in stress situations they do, and it can make the difference between health and disease, or sometimes life and death. A study by the London School of Hygiene and Tropical Medicine investigated the exercise patterns of a group of healthy people and those of 232 participants who suffered heart attacks. Only 11 percent of the heart patients had been in the habit of exercising strenuously, compared with 26 percent of the control group.

If you are sitting there wondering what kind of physical condition you yourself are in, there are some very simple tests you can take to find out. First, sit there another five minutes, without any kind of physical activity that amounts to anything, then take your pulse. The easiest way to do it, for most people, is not by wrist, but by pressing a thumb into the side of the neck to rest against the carotid artery. Check the beat against a sweep second hand for a full sixty seconds. If your heart at rest beats eighty times a minute or more, you are not in good condition. Sixty beats a minute, or fewer, is good. A little above seventy is average. Take the pulse four or five times in different resting situations to reach an average—there will be some variation, probably. To discover how your heart reacts to exertion, take some fairly strenuous concentrated exercise, rest a couple of minutes, then start checking your pulse to see how quickly it returns to normal.

A standard exertion test used by cardiologists is called the Masters two-step. The subject is asked to ascend and descend a nine-inch high step for a minute and a half while plugged into a cardiograph. If his reactions show abnormalities, the doctor will want to do some further testing.

Dr. Cooper, the aerobics man, does not think the heartbeat tests are definitive enough. His laboratory tests involve running the subject on a treadmill while wearing electrodes from a cardiograph attached to the chest and breathing into a device which measures consumption of oxygen. For the many subjects unable to get to such equipment he suggests running (or a combination of running and walking) twelve minutes to see how far you can go—after being checked out by your doctor.

A man under fifty who makes only one mile in the twelve minutes, and a woman who makes only three quarters of a mile, is in poor condition, in Cooper's judgment.

Dr. Cooper's remedial exercise regimen starts mildly for the out-of-shape, and gradually builds up to a program which can be accomplished in as little time, he says, as half an hour per day, depending on the exercise form chosen. In order of effectiveness he recommends: running, swimming, bicycling at a rapid rate (about twenty miles per hour), walking at three miles per hour or more, running in place, then games such as handball, squash and basketball; tennis and golf are too intermittent to do much good.

Running is Cooper's own favorite workout. The first benefits, according to his regular runners, are emotional repose and untroubled sleep, but Cooper has found considerable evidence that his programs also protect people against a number of common ailments. His reasoning, again, is that developing the lungs so they can get more oxygen into the blood stream—and from there into the body tissues—both increases the supply of blood throughout the body (a well-conditioned man will carry in his veins as much as a quart more blood than one who is out of condition) and enlarges the arterial system which carries it. One positive benefit occurs in blood pressure, which usually lowers with physical conditioning. Another occurs in the digestive system. A number of ulcer patients in his program have shown improvement, and Cooper's thesis is that not only does the psychological relaxation of running help by releasing pent-up aggression, but that conditioned people generally produce less acid in their stomachs. For individuals with respiratory problems, he believes greater improvement results from careful exercise than from the old regimens of rest. And in adult diabetes, the amount of insulin required can usually be reduced by a conditioning program. It was also Dr. Cooper who published, in *Aerospace Medicine,* his observations that exercise sometimes reduces interocular tension and thus helps in the insidious disease of open angle glaucoma.

The organ most drastically affected by exercise is, of course, the heart. This essential muscle suffers when its blood supply is cut down by narrowing arteries. Careful, regular exercise leads to the growth of extra capillary routes which help supply the heart with blood that the clogged main arteries can no longer deliver in sufficient quantity. As a result, people who exercise regularly have fewer heart attacks, and better survive the ones they do suffer.

But unless it is carefully paced, exercise has its hazards too, and many doctors decry the widespread fad today of jogging. The problem is overdoing: too far, too fast, too soon. This is common in highly competitive people, especially if they slip out of their age groups in the search for companions in exercise. They try to run faster than their rivals, even if the rivals are younger and in better shape. Some of them don't even need rivals: they will compete against themselves, pushing to make it around the block five seconds faster than yesterday. The result can be a coronary, sometimes fatal. In fact, it has been established that a fast walk of about three miles distance is almost as beneficial as jogging.

The story of one heart attack victim who attributes his survival to the benefits of exercise can be read in detail in a book called *Running Scared** by Tex Maule, a writer and editor for the magazine *Sports Illustrated*. At the time of his attack Maule was fifty-one years old and in reasonably good physical condition—he had never before had a hint of heart trouble, and for some time had been exercising fifteen minutes or so a day, a combination of calisthenics and running in place in his Manhattan apartment. Nevertheless, his coronary was a massive one, sending him to a hospital for a six-thousand-dollar stay, including much time on the intensive care ward.

Upon emerging, he was warned by his physician against exercise, as well as against smoking and drinking. He found this advice difficult to take, and finally, after gaining a lot of weight, he instead began jogging, with the help and encouragement of other joggers, as persuasive a group of missionaries as exists. It was not easy for him. In the nature of their work, most magazine writers come into the office late, leave late, and travel a lot, and as a result are difficult to ensnare into any regular routine, including that of exercising. He took months to come around, painful months. In time, however, Maule was running more than six miles, five days each week, and feeling better than he ever had.

When this kind of medical improvement can be wrought, despite a doctor's advice, on a magazine writer, it is particularly interesting to another of that waning profession, such as the author.

Which leads me into the subject of my own personal prescription for regular exercise, which I was a long time in coming to, like most middle-aged Americans.

Even in my twenties I found winter hard to take. I caught many colds and had a general sensation of being run down, and the older I got the harder it became

*Saturday Review Press, 1972.

to fend off the February syndrome, although in summer, with the usual modicum of outdoor life, things were better. At first, like many others, I resolved when fall came to continue the mild exertions of summer in a gymnasium at lunch time. I lined up a couple of friends to play court games with.

It started well. This was more concentrated exercise than pruning trees or paddling about on a rubber raft, and it also made for a good diverting lunchtime once or twice a week. But then came complications of winter holidays, travel, and work emergencies, and the schedule began to falter. The partners, including me, began to have to telephone each other and cancel out. In the end we found ourselves too often sitting partnerless in the steam room, a Gehenna that does little for health except for softening the beard and impressing one with the grossness of other out-of-shape bodies.

Then, while leafing through a magazine one day about seven years ago, I came across an advertisement by an insurance company urging me to write in for their exercise booklet. On impulse I did, and pinned the forthcoming chart up on the inside of the door of my clothes closet. In the morning I began to spend— and still spend—fifteen minutes doing various physical gyrations. I later sent away for the report of the President's Commission on Physical Fitness, with its more complete and slightly more rigorous recommendations.

All the exercises are combinations of isotonic exercises and stress exercises: first there is limbering up, then some exhaustion. They are all, of course, a terrible bore, but not quite so much so as that stale feeling in midwinter that one suffers without them. Although the sterner physical fitness masters scorn the isotonics, or at best, tolerate them, I've come to place some value on them. In isotonics, as in basketball or dancing, there is the pleasure and competence that come from increasing one's agility—the ability to turn quickly, twist, handle oneself under pressures that sometimes catch one off balance. When I was thirty years old, I couldn't touch my toes. Now that I can, quite a few years later, I think everyone should, frequently.

And I am moving on to finer things, although I have not yet worked up to the stringent rigors of the year-round aerobic program. Even my brief daily workout has slowed my pulse a dozen beats a minute. As a result, when I'm tired there is usually a cause.

And when a physical challenge comes my way, there is something inside me to respond to it, something that was not there before. It is there when I have to dash to catch the subway; when one of my children teases me into a chase across a beach; and when in summer I get interested in testing myself against Dr. Cooper's standards.

It is apparent to me that the benefits are more than merely physical. When I eat, it is with a lively appetite. A ride on the commuter train at the end of the day isn't soaked in that drained weariness: it is just another journey, as in the morning.

Nevertheless, anyone who gives more than fifteen minutes a day to exercise is likely, I've found, to smile at my minimal investment. They are probably correct. I usually run the equivalent of no more than half a mile daily. Almost worse, at least in my own eyes, is the fact that it's all run within the confines of my bedroom. This is, of course, deliberate. I know very well that if I did my running outdoors I'd miss lots of days. I'm damned if I'll charge into a northeast wind in the middle of January, and under my present system, when a heat wave strikes I can exercise with the air conditioner going.

But sometimes I wonder. And every once in a while, on a nice October afternoon out in the country, I put on my sweat shirt and soft shoes and take off up a dirt road I know.

Conditions are of course ideal. There is the smell of autumn leaves in the nippy air, and no neighbors to come to their windows to stare; there aren't even any dogs to bark and chase me (a common hazard in suburban running). But there is more to it than that.

What makes it so good? Am I ventilating emotions generated by profound primordial instincts of fear and flight—instincts I somehow share with the antelope and the ibex, and all those other animals whose survival is dependent on speed? Theoretically at least, this is part of it, yes. But my sensations do not feel like fear, or what I think of as fear. Fear, for me, is an unpleasant emotion that I deal with either by trying to think it away, or by executing certain deliberate and highly nonphysical plans. I fear the tax man when April comes, and quell the fear by reminding myself I have survived other Aprils. I fear old age, and so I open a savings account or invest modestly in what I hope is a growth stock. Perhaps fear is different in an antelope— and better. Perhaps he never feels so alive as when he is running for his life. Assuming, of course, that he makes it.

I, at any rate, chugging my way up that dirt road, am making it, and what I feel is not fear as I know it, but exhilaration; jubilance. By God I am covering ground at last! This is for me.

Then the next day it rains, and I go back to that worn spot on my bedroom rug.

There's nothing quite like running several miles a day outdoors, so do it if you can—but don't underestimate the time and determination it takes; it helps to be either a person of leisure or something of a zealot, and preferably both. Maule admitted, for example, that his six miles a day ate up most of three hours, if he included getting to the locker room first, and showering and getting back to the office again afterward.

Two of my favorite writers had very different approaches to conditioning. The late Robert Benchley had a couch in his room at the Royalton Hotel in Manhattan, a piece of furniture which he used to call The Track. Once in a while he'd say, "I guess I'll do a couple of laps around the track," and lie down on it. That great man died at age fifty-six of a cerebral hemorrhage. P. G. Wodehouse in 1919 happened across a calisthenics routine in a newspaper, and did his daily dozen well into his nineties.

DIET

One presumed benefit of exercise that you had better not count on, especially if you are over thirty, is loss of weight. Burning off calories through sheer physical exertion is not easy. Skiing across country on a really cold day may help, but you will come back to the lodge with such a raging hunger that your efforts are promptly undone by the solid lunch you eat. In golf, eighteen holes of exercise are easily cancelled out by a neat scotch in the locker room afterward.

In short, one's weight depends less on output than on intake: it is not insufficient exercise, but oversufficient food—particularly certain kinds of food—that makes so many Americans overweight.

We tend to think of obesity as a physical condition, or even a personal trait, rather than a form of illness. In itself it is never fatal, and any amateur can diagnose it. It remains for most, nevertheless, a disease, and one that is peculiarly difficult to cure.

It is also a stress disease. First, it creates stress. Obese people are, by the stern standards of our society, unattractive, and this simple fact hampers not only their relations with other people, but also their feelings about themselves. In addition, the extra poundage places them under a continuous physical strain. Every time they climb the stairs or run for a bus it is as if they were carrying a sack of books—all their physical equipment has to work harder to move the load. As a result, obesity in an individual is often eventually joined by other ailments—kidney disease, diabetes, high blood pressure, gall bladder problems, or heart trouble. No direct causative link has yet been established between cardiovascular disease and obesity, but most nutritionists assume that it exists, simply because the two go together so often.

Obesity is not only a cause of stress but, also, very often, a result of it. Certain people react to pressure by overeating, just as certain others react by over-working, and yet others by reaching for a cigarette. Indeed, the dieter and the person who wants to stop smoking face a similar dilemma. The strains that self-denial exerts on them are hideously exacerbated by the fact that the thing they are trying to cut out of their lives happens to be the one thing they have relied on for years to get them through stress of all kinds. "How can I ever go through this agony without a cigarette!" wonders the new ex-smoker in despair on his or her first day, and the dieter thinks, "I could stand the hunger, I could stand anything, if they'd only let me have an *Oh Henry* bar!"

What makes people overeat? Early training may be one answer. Dr. Stanley Schachter, in the anthology *Neurophysiology and Emotion,* edited by David C. Glass (Rockefeller University Press, 1967), describes the plight of the newborn infant in these words:

> Wholly at the mercy of its feelings, it screams when it is uncomfortable or in pain or frightened or hungry. Whether it is comforted, soothed, fondled, or fed has little to do with the state of its feelings, but depends entirely on the ability and willingness of its mother or nurse to recognize the proper cues. If she is experienced, she will comfort when the baby is frightened, soothe him when he is chafed, feed him when he is

hungry, and so on. If inexperienced, her behavior may be completely inappropriate to the child's state. Most commonly, perhaps, the compassionate but bewildered mother will feed her child at any sign of distress.

It is precisely this state of affairs that the analyst Hilde Bruch suggests is at the heart of chronic obesity. She describes such cases as characterized by confusion between intense emotional states and hunger. During childhood, she presumes, these patients have not been taught to discriminate between hunger and such states as fear, anger, and anxiety. If this is so, the patients may be labeling almost any state of arousal as hunger.

So when obese people say they are hungry, they may not mean the same thing that normal people do when they say they are hungry. The obese may mean simply that they are upset in some fashion—and they respond in the way their mothers taught them to respond, by eating.

Some researchers have decided that fat people have different kinds of fat cells, and more of them, than thin people, and it has been speculated that, again, feeding experiences in infancy may be largely to blame. A normal child possesses some twenty-five billion fat cells, but a baby whose anxious mother regularly overfeeds it may go on to develop two or three times as many as that, all of them ready and waiting to absorb the food eaten in the form of excess poundage. Thus obesity, through training, can become a physiological need as well as a psychological one.

How much *should* people weigh? This is a question that each generation answers a little differently: Lillian Russell had one opinion, Twiggy another, and neither has much basis in actual body requirements. "The simple fact is that some people function at their best with a relatively greater amount of fat tissue, which is normal for them. . . ." wrote Hilde Bruche. "It is an amazing paradox that our culture, with its great flexibility and liberal ideas, attempts to superimpose *one* form of body build on those whom nature has endowed differently."

The best-known analysis of natural variations in physique is Dr. William Sheldon's. In 1940 he published a study on four thousand college students—all men—and was able to sort them into three categories:

Endomorphs—large stomachs, general softness of body, small bones and muscles.
Mesomorphs—spare, hard, resistant builds, big muscles and bones.
Ectomorphs—thin all around, with small muscles, but large heads.

Sheldon went on to try to relate these physical characteristics to personality traits. He found considerable correlation between endomorphs and the love of comfort. They were given to sociability, gluttony, ample relaxation, slow reactions, even temper, and tolerance. Mesomorphs he found more vigorous and aggressive. They wanted to dominate, and often succeeded. Ectomorphs, by comparison with the other two types, were inhibited, self-conscious, solitary, fearful, and generally reserved.

But does one's body frame dictate one's character, or is it the other way around? "The other way around," is the determined answer of many Americans—with the result that the middle-aged women in this country in a recent twenty-year period willed themselves lighter, by an average of ten pounds. They accomplished this by dieting, in a period when the average middle-age male was gaining six pounds.

Should you join the dieters? is the next question. And if so, how, specifically, should you proceed?

For most of this century Americans have worried

increasingly about their weight, until by now one would think they had the problem figured out, so many and so varied have been the attempts at a solution. In the twenties and thirties the villain was commonly thought, even in medical circles, to be an endocrine malfunction, and thyroid shots and pills were plunged into countless thousands of patients, particularly into plump children, although there was little result in the vast majority of cases. More recently the fads have been less medical, more purely promotional. There may be almost as many reducing books on the market as cookbooks. Perhaps the most notorious was one published in 1961 which maintained that calories did not count, and which several million overweight Americans virtually devoured. Its author, a doctor, recommended regular dosing with safflower oil, and made the mistake of naming just which brands to buy. This brought a federal conviction for mail fraud, violations of federal food and drug regulations, and conspiracy.

In the same general period Mead Johnson & Co. invented a product, then hired a computer to find a name for it, and Metrecal was born, to be seized upon by millions of overweight Americans as their salvation. There was nothing at all harmful in Metrecal, according to nutritionists. It was a blend of casein, sugar, vitamins, minerals, and a little oil. It helped boost Mead Johnson's stock from 55 in 1959 to 202 in 1961, while it was catching on. But like later versions of liquid diet that have superceded it, it was very glubby stuff which few could take as a steady diet.

Famous and infamous food fads have ranged from the Mayo diet* consisting mostly of grapefruit, eggs, and bacon, to the Drinking Man's Diet, with such variations as the whipped-cream-and-martini diet and the so-called Eskimo diet—nothing but fish and animal

*Unconnected with the Mayo Clinic.

fats. Then there is the Zen Buddhist Macrobiotic diet, based on brown rice, which is said not only to slim but to cure various illnesses, and improve the memory. Perhaps the most appealing idea of all came in 1964, when a leading European medical journal, *Münchener Medizinische Wöchenschrift*, published a report by Dr. Heinz Humplik of Vienna stating that some common foods, because of the labor involved in digesting them, actually burn up more calories than they add. If a person of ordinary metabolism ingested a hard-boiled egg he would not add eighty calories to his or her pouch, as had always been presumed, but would subtract twelve—and he still would have had the satisfaction of eating the egg. The article caused appreciable commotion among the overweight in Germany, although the overweight in Germany are not so excitable as the overweight in America. Then the news crossed the Atlantic. A fashion magazine, *Harper's Bazaar*, trumpeted, "Eat, Eat, Eat Your Pounds Away. . . . If you ate four hard-boiled eggs, you would lose, just because you ate them, forty-eight calories (equivalent to a 100-yard dash)."

At last Frederick J. Stare, Chairman of the Department of Nutrition at Harvard's School of Public Health, got in touch with the director of Germany's Institute of Nutrition, and received a sigh of a reply. There was indeed a Dr. Heinz Humplik but the implication was *nein,* he was not in the running for the Nobel Prize. His nonsensical report had somehow slipped by the editorial board of *Münchener Medizinische Wöchenschrift* and into print. And so sank another fond delusion.

If you are a person with a weight problem,* but

---

*You probably know just from looking in the mirror whether you are overweight or not, but there are several validating tests you can take in case you aren't sure—and getting on the scales is not necessarily one of them.

want to steer clear of fads, your first step is to seek assistance from a reputable general practitioner. He or she will examine you—and depending on the findings, may even advise against dieting. For example a high protein diet (about which, more later) can play havoc on anyone with a kidney malfunction; or, in some cases, heart problems, or during pregnancy. Some of the most effective diets do, by the very nature of things, upset the balance of nutritional intake, and if your balance is delicate you should know it.

More probably, however, your general health is satisfactory, and the doctor will proceed with somewhat glummer advice: eat a little less, but without disturbing dietary balance. Calories do count, you will be told. You may further be advised that the average American intake of calories per day is about three thousand, but that almost anyone who doesn't dig ditches hard all day can get along very well on 2,000. Leave a little on the plate. Don't try to take off more than two pounds a month, but keep at it. Remember that a pound of body fat equals 350 calories.

It will be a fairly morose session: the same as being told to get more exercise, but worse. Actually, the doctor might have better luck talking you into giving up cigarettes or alcohol. With both of these the break can be complete, the habit can be banished altogether.

But not in the case of food. One does have to eat. The same drives that have made the patient overeat in

---

First, measure the thickness of a fold of skin at the back of your upper arm, the triceps. It should measure no more than one inch, including subcutaneous fat. Next, try pinching the skin just below one of your shoulder blades between thumb and forefinger. It, likewise, should not exceed an inch. Finally pass on to the area of flesh just below the rib cage, which, in theory, should also be only an inch or less in fold. You may well pass the first two tests but fail the third one: poor posture, or an inherited tendency in body type, can cause the thickening to begin here first.

the past will be operating daily in the future. Consigning the average American patient to a steady sensation of hunger very seldom works if what the doctor is recommending entails no change besides merely cutting down.

Weight, however, can be taken off most people by a variety of means, one of which is based on a chemical trick of sorts. When the body piles up excess calories in the form of fat reserves, these reserves must be brought into action in order to burn them off. A balanced diet does not usually accomplish this, again, unless it is a most radically diminished balanced diet, and long term, nearly impossible to sustain.

What does move the fat out of storage and into action is a marked reduction in the kind of calories contained in carbohydrate foods—the worst of them being sugar, alcohol, bread, candy, cereal, potatoes, pasta, and certain vegetables and fruits—with reliance for energy instead on high-protein calories—lean meat, poultry, fresh fish (but not shellfish), eggs, and some cheeses.

The high protein food apparently is the activator in weight loss, the spark plug that makes the engine start up. It seems to stimulate metabolism to burn food faster, and it also draws forth the fat stored in the cells and converts it into carbohydrates, especially sugar, that the body does require. Some fatty acids are left to be disposed of through the kidneys, which is why some of the doctors who recommend this diet also recommend that their patients drink a great deal of water—and which is also why defective kidneys must bar you from use of this diet.

You can consume a fairly full quota of calories on a high-protein diet, yet it is not much easier to tolerate long term than standard calorie cutting. A total ban on bread, fruit, vegetables, and sweets gets to be a drag after the novelty dwindles. The interior glow auguring accomplishment soon becomes more like an interior glower. Despite the calories, you still feel hungry. Besides, your mouth tastes bad.

But the good thing about the high-protein diet is that it can be let up, usually, after a week at most. By then the stored fats are usually flowing into consumption, and some carbohydrate can be brought back to cheer you up. These are mostly the "innocent" carbohydrates, however. And the truly obese will have to postpone, perhaps forever, any but artificial sweeteners—sugar can turn off the fat-burning process.

The high-protein dieter must still be concerned with calories, of course, but this is less a matter of grinding deprivation than a kind of balancing act. In most diet books you will find lists of calorie counts for various foods. Apart from several high ratings for some of the green vegetables, the list contains few surprises, and the gross offenders continue to be fats and oils of all kinds, as well as sweets and alcohol—all those luxuries.

You will also find you do slowly lose your taste— or at least, your desperate yearning—for certain sumptuous dishes. Giving up sugar is difficult for most of us, having been brought up in a century and a country where sugar consumption has advanced at almost the rate of the national debt. Too many of us have had a Coke-and-Pepsi-candy-bar childhood, becoming dependent on the quick jab of energy zapped into our blood by such sweets, an energy which wears off very quickly as the blood-sugar level dives back down, stimulating a longing yen to have another, an endless, fruitless fluctuation. But the sweets habit, like the butter habit, mercifully does wear off, when fought.

To survive dieting, you simply have to permit yourself an occasional deviation, and most good diet books recognize the fact. Even the more potent carbohydrates can be nibbled now and then. One evening I had dinner at an excellent Chinese restaurant on Manhattan's Third Avenue with one of the most eminent of obesity doctors, who himself has a weight problem well under control. He explained to me that this was a place where any of his patients could dine, because he has induced the management to cut back the starchy content of its menu. It was a superb meal, and my companion started it off with a Chivas Regal and soda—but only one, it should be noted. This doctor has also worked things out with one of Manhattan's first-rate Italian restaurants, so that his patients on an evening out now have a choice of two cuisines, neither of which will cause repentance on the scales the next day.

It is when they dine in restaurants, of course, or at the homes of friends, that dieters suffer some of their worst torments, and so frequently abandon all self-control. The other occasion is late at night, at home. You are alone, the only one awake in the house, and if it is some inner anxiety that drives you to overeat, the loneliness helps warm up the engine.

There are many little tricks to ease the pangs of dieting. Banishing certain food combinations—no butter with bread, for instance—is basic, and easy. Some dieters deliberately eat lean all week, then let go a little on the weekend to reward themselves, and this can work well if the letting go does not turn into a culinary stampede. There are many trim people who deliberately keep so busy at the office that they skip lunch. I frequently cross the street to a good delicatessen and have a tomato sandwich (hold the mayo) with a lot of pickles and two black coffees, and am amazed by how much work I get done in the afternoon. The late Arthur Vining Davis, the business genius of the Aluminum Company of America—its first employee, and eventually president and chairman—said he never ate lunch, and his colleagues could not discover, hard as they tried, that he smuggled any food into the office. Lean and spare, he continued to command ALCOA until he was ninety years old, then went to Florida to buy much of Dade County, and finally died at ninety-five, a rich and slender man.

One popular method of reducing just now is to join a club of dieters who have banded together, fusing their individual determination into a great mutual resolve. Weight Watchers and other such organizations provide calorie guides, frequent changes of motivation, and a great deal of encouragement in the old revival meeting style, with mutual confession of dietary sins a prominent feature. It is wise in such groups, however, to be on guard against a spirit of excessive rivalry. In the shedding of pounds, as in everything else, driving competitiveness can lead to anxiety, which in turn provokes in most dieters that awful craving for food. But mutual support from fellow sufferers, whether the problem is obesity or tuberculosis, is very useful, as described in the next chapter.

Another kind of support, that given by a medical authority who charges you for it, may be useful also—and in some cases of obesity, essential. A hundred pounds of excess weight is a serious matter, and anyone who does not suggest the help of a specialist for the grossly obese is being unrealistic.

This is a delicate area, because it involves diet doctors and we've all been warned about diet doctors. What most of them do is administer diuretics to drain the water out of their patients' bodies, then peddle pills or plunge in injections that drug the appetite for a while—until the effect wears off. These druggist-doctors are quacks at best, and at worst are purveyors of pills that can be dangerous. They are fairly easy to recognize. Stay away from them.

But in some of the larger cities there are a handful of medical specialists seriously at work on the obesity problem, in an attempt to help severely afflicted men and women. Some time ago, one of these doctors began treating a man who had spent most of his life being really fat—grossly, miserably so—then going on diets, only to cave in and return to the feed pen like an addled heifer longing for its mother.

This man is a professional at the top of his field, and prosperous (which is fortunate, because losing weight with a top specialist is an expensive process). He is about five feet ten inches tall, and at the age of forty-seven weighed 290 pounds and was gaining. He heard about the diet doctor from his general practitioner.

He was decidedly encouraged by his first appointment. There was no medical sell. Instead he found himself arguing hard to prove he possessed the determination necessary to do something drastic about his poundage. Once the doctor was convinced, she had her assistant give him a medical examination of more than ordinary completeness, from cardiogram, to body chemistry studies, to a very detailed taking of his history. Special attention was paid to the way his body handled sugar; a four-hour glucose tolerance test was given.

On the second visit, the test results before her, the doctor enunciated some premises, and made some promises. First, she admitted him to the company of most of her patients: his blood sugar level, like theirs, was erratic, at times plunging so low that it caused not only intense hunger but a kind of overall physiological depression as well. This was one reason he had never been able to stick to conventional diets—they did not permit him to eat enough to keep his blood sugar level up. Thus his condition, in her opinion, was to some degree a metabolic problem—not simply a matter of eating too much, but of eating too much of the wrong food.

The diet which this particular doctor prescribed, she promised, would neither deny him all his favorite foods, nor inflict upon him a steady, gnawing hunger. He could eat as much lean meat, fish or fowl as he liked. But no refined sugar, probably ever again. Then she sent him home to a week of high-protein eating.

The week was not easy but he got through it, cheered on by daily success on the scales.

When he returned to the doctor at the end of the week, he got his first reward. She asked him what his favorite foods were and took care to work a few of them into his coming week's schedule. Others she introduced in later weeks, all part of an intricate system designed to help people like himself go on losing, slowly but surely, till at last their weight reaches normal—and then to keep it there. At this visit she warned him that his weight loss would be very gradual and that he was embarking on an eating program that he would probably have to subscribe to forever. For him there would be no vacations, no retrieval crash diets. But he would not be hungry, and there would be the rewards, not only on the menu but in a new feeling of well-being.

That was fifteen months ago. Since then he has lost ninety-five pounds, and is still losing. Some months the system goes like clockwork—punctually each week, two pounds disappear. Then he seems to reach a plateau, and it gets more difficult. When this happens the diet is talked over with his doctor, and readjusted, and then it begins to work again.

He continues to see her weekly. Her personal attention is of course an important motivator—and so is the sixty dollars he pays her each visit. But what matters is that it works. "God, I feel good!" he said to me not long ago. "I'm *not* hungry all the time. I eat good food. I can even drink a little. When I used to go on a diet, in the old days, it murdered me—my will power, my morale, my work, everything went to pieces. This one I can move around in—and still I lose.''

Calories are not our only food problem. We now know that cholesterol is connected with heart disease; that raw shellfish from unclean waters can cause hepatitis; that virtually all processed foods like flour or rice contain small amounts of such inadvertent additives as mouse droppings.

Cholesterol remains one of the biggest scares. Almost all doctors today accept the thesis that cholesterol is connected with cardiovascular disease. But what *is* the connection? In particular, what is the connection between disease and cholesterol in the diet? No one is yet sure, and many suspect that cholesterol is only a symptom, not a cause. Some people have high cholesterol blood levels—and much heart trouble—but eat very little fat. Other people eat food extremely high in cholesterol, yet their blood levels remain low and their hearts healthy.*

Considerations like these draw people to health food stores, or sometimes lead them to start their own vegetable garden. This is hard work, and of course you need a yard, but for many people there is something inordinately satisfying about having a vegetable patch. Picked just before cooking, the vegetables really taste, especially young peas, corn, lima beans, and asparagus. You can grown things that are hard to find in

*The reason may lie with the lipoproteins in the blood. There are two types of lipoproteins, known as high-density and low-density. People with elevated levels of *high*-density lipoproteins are thought to be able to consume saturated fats more safely because they possess a natural broom that cleans the plaque from their arteries. Those with elevated *low*-density lipoprotein scores have to be more careful: the plaque accumulates.

grocery stores, or else very expensive, such as raspberries and tarragon. Running a vegetable garden is excellent exercise, and the cost is low. It is good for the spirit, too.

CHAPTER 9

Altering Your Response to Stress: Psychotherapy, Drugs, Support Groups, Meditation, Biological Feedback, Hypnosis

The subtlest of the sciences is still psychology: the functioning of man's mind, or, to use a soulful word, his psyche. Its most eminent figure, of course, was Sigmund Freud (1859–1939). Today he is widely regarded as a prophet, and deservedly so, but it is important to remember that he arrived at his position not so much by sheer intellectual formulation as through his practical daily work as a physician. It was his mission to substantially improve his patients' emotional condition, and to do this he was willing to venture into forbidden areas. In his youth he even had an interlude of involvement with that mood-altering drug, cocaine, but dropped it in horror when a friend became addicted and died. In Freud's old age, suffering torments from cancer of the jaw under that respectable beard, he resisted drugs until the very end—but never gave up his cigars.

Analytical psychiatry in Freud's own time was regarded by most of the public as a form of mental safecracking—an invasion of privacy, and anti-Christian to boot. Yet its basic premise is simply that people are individuals, each driven by the intricate motives created by his or her specific experiences back into infancy.

Fundamental to this premise was Freud's concept of the unconscious mind. Under the level of awareness, of conscious thought and conniving, he taught, lies a vast area of sleeping memory. The unconscious contains the relics of everything that has ever happened to us, original sensations, hopes and fears, infantile worries and adolescent shocks, pleasures and traumas. From its depths rise strong currents that can stir the surface to storms of depression, even to psychotic typhoons. The only way a person really can understand his own emotional weather is to examine what is down there, event by event, sunken ship by sunken ship.

Freud evolved the process by which this can be done over many years, revising his own course more than once. He started in 1885, four years after entering practice in Vienna, when he went to Paris to study with Jean Charcot, who had begun to penetrate humanity's depths through hypnosis. Hypnosis had been around for a couple of centuries at least, and at one period was generally assumed to work by magnetism. In the late 1700s, in France, F. A. Mesmer was its best-known practitioner, and he made passes with his metals over many ailing people. He was finally cast into disrepute after King Louis XVI appointed one of those committees of V.I.P.'s to look into the matter, including Lavoisier, discoverer of oxygen, Benjamin Franklin, U.S. ambassador and electrical expert, and Doctor J. I. Guillotin, inventor of the guillotine. The committee disapproved. But hypnosis was a fact of life, and continued to be studied—by, among others, Mrs. Mary Baker Eddy, who investigated the matter with a New England practitioner named Phineas Quimby before going on to found the Christian Science Church.

Charcot, Freud's early teacher, was neither a faithhealer nor a charlatan, but a serious medical scholar and practicing neurologist and it was from his lectures on hypnosis that Freud caught his first real glimpse of the unconscious mind. He carried this glimpse back to Vienna with him, and with Dr. Joseph Breuer made a now famous study of hysteria, using Charcot's technique of hypnosis. Then he set about working out his own method of exploration, better than hypnosis because his patients' full awareness could be brought into play. It was called free association. The patients did it themselves, with the psychiatrist acting as guide and emotional fulcrum.

Freudian theory holds that sexual conflicts in infancy and childhood are the basic factors in personality development, and that unless these conflicts are resolved at the time, they perpetuate themselves in later life in elaborate frameworks of neurotic behavior; the patient, in psychoanalysis, attempts to recapture these pivotal early experiences, work them through successfully, and thus cure his or her neurosis.

Today all psychiatrists acknowledge their debt to Freud's general approach, but many have reservations about the specifics. Is it sexuality that is at the core of our problems, or is it society—our relations with other people? Are our problems innate, part of the emotional and biological structure we are born with, or do we create them, through the tactics we develop to defend ourselves, and which must themselves be defended by still other tactics? Above all, what should we do about it? Should we reach back and relive the long repressed traumas of infancy, or face up to the here and now? Does "insight" really cure? And what is a cure?—What do we want to become?

From orgone therapy to transactional analysis, the various schools of thought today all answer these questions differently. The followers of Wilhelm Reich believe that full genital sexuality is the mark of emotional health, and that neurosis begins when the incestuous longings of early childhood come up against the repressive strictures of society. The Karen Horney group, on the other hand, regards sex as secondary, and holds that the original problem is the clash between feelings of hostility and dependency. In infancy, the future neurotic finds himself at the mercy of his mother, and hates her for it—yet he cannot put his hatred into action because he *is* so dependent. Threatened in this way by his own conflicting impulses, he proceeds to develop strategies, techniques of behavior that reflect not his natural and spontaneous feelings, but his simple need for safety. He may develop into a person who is unduly compliant ("moving toward" others), or unduly aggressive ("moving against" them), or he may, in effect, attempt to evade the whole problem by "moving away"—isolating himself, suppressing his emotions, restricting his wants so he can be independent of others. Normal people also use these three strategies, Dr. Horney said, but use them flexibly and realistically in the service of the self. Neurotics, impelled by their basic fear, are rigid and driven, and their compulsive tactics stifle their own development. The purpose of therapy is to change these compulsive patterns and free the personality.

Growth and self-realization are heavily emphasized by most modern schools of psychotherapy. Existential therapists see personality as ever-developing, and like to quote Kierkegaard: "To exist does not mean to be finished, to exist means to become." Erik Erikson postulates eight stages in a person's life, each with its basic challenge which, if met and mastered, allows the person to pass on to the next stage, in the process gradually evolving a rich and meaningful individuality.

The technique of psychotherapy, as practiced today, varies widely. Classical Freudian analysis remains available—for the average patient, five sessions a week over a period of several years—but it is frighteningly expensive, and there are some patients who cannot afford it emotionally: their inner problems are so severe that plumbing the depths is more than they can stand. Its rate of "cures," most analysts admit, is rather low. Other schools of therapy believe that faster results are achieved by focusing on current problems more than on infantile conflicts, and these therapists are apt to play more active roles in treatment—commenting, interpreting, encouraging. At the far end of the scale is the kind of treatment that omits analysis in favor of what amounts to behavioral conditioning. Dr. Joseph Wolpe of Temple University claims that behavioral therapy improves or cures nine out of ten patients who give it a real chance, compared with maybe six out of ten for psychoanalysis—and he says it does the job a great deal faster. The reason? Anxiety, writes Dr. Wolpe, "is based on learning at a subcortical level of neural integration, which is not likely to be undone merely because thinking, a cortical affair, has changed." Analytic therapy, in his opinion, misses the real mark.

In any case, patients usually find that talking in the presence of the therapist, lifting the veil, makes them feel better almost at once—and crying even more so. This is called venting. One doesn't have to be a psychiatrist to qualify as an audience, of course; a tolerant friend may suffice; and for centuries clergymen filled the role, and many of them still do. But the impersonality of the psychotherapist, the professionalism, the skilled prompting, the therapeutic intent, provide a great advantage. A disadvantage is the costliness, again, but that enforces the impersonality, and it also makes the process more purposeful for patients: it gives them, to put it bluntly, a financial motive for recovery.

So far, it is the general value of psychiatry that we have been discussing. What about its value in treating physical stress symptoms? Does it work? The answer is a modified yes.

It works, but it works better in some conditions than others. Disorders of the digestive tract, such as ulcers and colitis, seem to be particularly responsive.

Hyperthyroidism may improve markedly in as few as six sittings. Asthma, on the other hand, can be quite slow to respond, perhaps because it usually starts in childhood and is more deeply ingrained in the patient's behavior.

In fact, when therapy fails to improve psychogenic physical symptoms, one of the commonest reasons is not that there is anything wrong with the therapy itself, but simply that it comes to bear too late in the game. Many diseases become evident only after years of silent and unsuspected growth, during which the patient feels in perfect health. From autopsy studies performed on U.S. soldiers killed in the Korean war, for instance, it has been learned that the average American male by the time he is in his mid-twenties possesses arteries already narrowed by deposits of cholesterol and other substances. Unfortunately, he doesn't know it, and in most cases won't know it for another twenty or thirty years, when he may suddenly be stricken by heart trouble or hypertension. And if the disease is psychogenic—the result of habitual responses to pressure—it isn't going to be easy to cure through psychotherapy. A fifty-year-old habit is hard to break.

Even with diseases that develop more rapidly, time is still important and all too often works against the patient. Psychotherapy is seldom the first choice of treatment. Everything else is tried instead—one drug, then another, then maybe a special diet, then surgery—all have their turn, and all may make you feel somewhat better, at least for a while. But if you become worse again, and psychotherapy is resorted to, six or seven years may have passed, and the physiological patterns are firmly rooted.

The same is true of emotional patterns in illness. With the passage of time, a chronic disease changes the mentality of its victims. They get used to it. They learn to live with it. And pretty soon, in many cases, they can no longer live without it. It excuses them from numerous obligations and challenges, and gains them attention and care. It works its way into their emotional economy and becomes a convenient and satisfying mechanism for expressing guilt and achieving expiation. "Secondary gain" is the official name of this game. In their heart of hearts, the people who play it no longer really want to get well, and psychotherapy cannot do much for them.

Therapists who handle a lot of psychosomatic cases emphasize several other points. One is that psychiatric treatment should be combined with standard medical treatment, the therapist and the family doctor collaborating together to solve the patient's physical problem. Therapy can actually aggravate symptoms temporarily, or alter them in other unexpected ways. Another is that therapy for a physical condition, as compared with the treatment of purely emotional problems, is sometimes surprisingly brief. It is not considered necessary or even desirable in most cases to try to recapture the experiences of infancy or the oedipal period. The focus is on the physical affliction itself, on uncovering the emotions that are causing it and then finding a better way of expressing these emotions. This can of course lead to new problems. People undergoing psychiatric treatment are often very hard to live with.

And in fact the therapist must not be in too big a hurry. Patients who express their feelings by getting sick do so because the feelings are dangerous to them. If they are pressed to release them fast, before they are ready, the result can be a mental breakdown.

True to Freud, every patient is different, and needs a different course of treatment.

Take the case of a man whose stress symptom is ulcers, for reasons that are almost a cliché. He has a boss who rides roughshod over him, and a wife who is too busy with her own career to comfort him. His children are even less predictable than the boss. The patient is not getting the things he needs out of life, and he resents it bitterly, and knows that he resents it, but what can he do? He is a man, not a child, and his only recourse is to go on struggling—swallow his resentment, go out and seize what fragments and shreds that he can, and play the game according to the established rules. He says to himself, "Sure I've got ulcers—who wouldn't, in my position?"

Compare him with a second ulcer patient—more or less the same age, same surroundings, in working life as well as personal life. But this one, unlike the first, does *not* understand why her stomach is hurting. The first patient's resentment may be curbed; but this woman isn't even aware of hers, just of that pain in her stomach. In the course of her life to date, what she has learned is how to absorb indignities, perhaps even developing the habit of courting them, without feeling much of anything emotionally.

Psychiatrists, surprisingly, will tell you that the second patient may respond more swiftly to treatment than the first. She needs to realize what is really going on inside her, and the shock of recognition may do the rest. If she can only uncover her true emotions—a process involving perhaps ten to twenty hours of therapy—then her stomach can relax, and she will be able to abandon her ulcer medication.

Maybe the trouble with the first patient is that he knows too much about himself, and his knowledge has become enmeshed, so to speak, in the disorder itself, has become a kind of hostage to it—a force that might have worked for his recovery, but instead is working against it.

Then, too, the course of therapy is affected by the nature of the inner feelings involved. If what the patient secretly wants is to be nurtured and cared for, for instance, it makes good sense for her to become aware of these feelings because a place *can* be found for them in modern society. In the process, she may not only heal her ulcer, she may also part company with her husband and start getting involved with the affectionate, easygoing guy in the next office. These may be drastic measures, but they are practical ones because they are capable of improving her life. But what if her repressed feelings are truly unacceptable—homicidal rage, for example? Then self-awareness isn't enough, and therapy will have to help the patient to change herself—a much more difficult task.

The psychiatric treatment of functional disease also gets complicated when it has to contend with adverse developments in the patient's outside world. Here is a case from the files of psychoanalyst Samuel Silverman of Brookline, Massachusetts, which also, incidentally, illustrates the constant shifting of balances between emotional and physical symptoms:

The patient, a pharmacist in his early sixties, originally came for psychiatric consultation because of deepening depression. At that time he presented no physical symptoms, though he revealed that ten years before, after experiencing rather prolonged easy fatigability, he had been examined by a physician who found "high blood pressure." Subsequent checkups revealed pressures in the range of 170 to 180–80 to 90. The patient was reassured by his physician and thereafter had no further physical complaints. He was the older of two siblings, his brother, now a successful lawyer, having been born when the patient was fourteen years old. For a long time the patient was an only child but, because parents were both busy in the family business, he was looked after by his maternal grandmother who spoiled him a great deal and would also frighten him with ghost stories and tales about his grandfather's death. He grew up to be a rather shy individual, sensitive, easily upset by losses, but a hard worker who put himself through pharmacy school and then went into business for himself. When he was not working, he would read extensively. He was married and had two grown sons.

The patient's depression clearly coincided with the finalization of plans for urban renewal which involved the area in which his pharmacy had been located for over thirty years. This had been his little "domain" where he ruled as a "benevolent neighborhood despot," being looked up to and admired for his considerate attitude toward his customers and for his obviously superior intellect. The early interviews were filled with many references to the traumatic effect the forced giving up of his business was having on him. It had also activated the involutional process, and this became part of his depressive tendencies. He thought that "everything" was over, that he could not get started again, and that he had made many terrible mistakes in the past. It was felt that a supportive approach was indicated in the treatment. This was done in the form of sympathetic listening, reassurance, exploration of the more optimistic possibilities in his reality situation, and emphasis on the positives in his past. This, together with the patient's ability to ventilate some of his more immediate hostile feelings, resulted in a lessening of the depression. At this point, the therapist had to be away for a month, and treatment was interrupted. Subsequently, the patient did not resume treatment, but called to say he continued to feel less depressed. Several months later, he arranged to come in for a "checkup," but arrived at the wrong time, waited an hour, and then left. A new appointment several weeks later was kept. At that time, he stated that his improvement was being maintained and that he had undertaken to start a new pharmacy in another section of the city. He indicated he was experiencing somatic reactions: "butterflies in the stomach and slight vertigo." He ascribed this to nervous tension at the prospect of "starting from scratch all over again after so many years." He did not return for further interviews, but about a month later, after finalizing rental and renovation plans for his new store, he had increasing symptoms of vertigo and then an episode of Stokes-Adams syncope [fainting]. He was hospitalized and a heart block with pulse rate of thirty to thirty-two per minute was discovered. On returning home, he had a number of syncopal attacks resulting in minor head injuries, despite a carefully worked out medical regimen, including increased doses of ephedrine. For a while he was restricted in his activities to a bedchair area.

Psychotherapy was resumed at this time. Depressive manifestations could again be noted, but this time they appeared in part to be secondary to the physical illness. His long-standing inferiority feelings, long defended against by his position as "king" in the old store, had been greatly activated by the uncertainties of his new venture, and now by the physical difficulties he had been experiencing. Confidence was at a low ebb, and there was marked anxiety. Superego reactions to all this were in the form of much self-blame, devaluation and guilt. The traumatic effect of his being dislocated from his old business had been reinforced by a second "shock wave"—the reality of having to start afresh in a new and strange setting. Once again, in the presence of an ambivalent but more positively weighted transference, a supportive approach was intensively employed. A most extensive airing of hostile thoughts and impulses was possible. Then after a month, the patient brought up highly traumatic childhood memories; when he was about six he had tried to get closer to his father, to have him show more affection. Time and again his father rudely and abruptly pushed him away, until the patient felt that he was not wanted or liked by his father. The recollections, many years repressed in this man of over sixty, were related with great emotion, and accompanied by bitter crying. Following these abreactive episodes he said: "I feel free, as if a burden had dropped off. I had been carrying this hate for so many years and now I feel as if I had made my peace with father." Following this, there was definite and increasing physical improvement. The patient was able to increase his activities and had no further syncopal attacks. His pulse rate became stabilized in the forties. There was renewed self-confidence, manifested by a growing interest and participation in the late-stage planning and developments in the new store.

Further psychotherapeutic work was in the direction of developing some further but limited insights into his basic emotional problems.

Some five years later, the patient had continued to feel well physically and had made his new store into a highly successful venture. He had been able to resume his formerly active life.*

Recoving from that drastic but necessary growing-up process, the rupture of childhood—making peace with one's parents, even a half century later—is what the greater part of psychiatry may be about, for most people.

DRUGS

In the early 1950s psychiatrists were presented with a very useful tool, the first psychotropic drugs, chemicals which enabled them to calm down their patients without sedating them. The drugs changed American life. Thanks to chlorprosmazine, countless mental patients who would otherwise have to be hospitalized could now live at home and even hold jobs, though they usually did need some out-patient therapy. And meeker, milder variations of these drugs proved of inestimable help to people who were not psychotic but merely anxious, depressed, overwrought, suffering the conventional strains and stresses of the culture. Unlike barbiturates or the even older drug, alcohol, the newer family of chemicals did not turn off the higher functions of the brain, did not dull the sharpness of the patient's insight.

The pills came to be used to ease the processes of everything from long-range trucking, to sex law suits, and professional football, and they were worth billions

*Samuel Silverman, *Psychological Aspects of Physical Symptoms*, Appleton-Century-Crofts, 1968.

a year to the pharmaceutical industry. Some of them quieted you down and some of them pepped you up, but what they all did when they worked well was to bring a calm kind of energy to their takers, making it easier to focus on the obtainable in life and to go after it with confidence and pleasure.

But they didn't always work well. In recent years public health officials have worried almost as much about these synthetics as about their poppyseed predecessors, and the remarkable extent to which people in our society have come to rely on mood-altering drugs of all kinds has been documented in many studies. One of these, completed for the New York State Addiction Control Commission, and including hard drugs, is particularly interesting because it concerns itself not with addicts, as we think of them, but simply with ordinary users in average American homes. The figures below were projected from interviews with a sizable sample of the 13,690,000 residents of New York State age fourteen or older in the years 1968-70. None of them were derelicts, flophouse residents, patients in hospitals, or homeless.

Barbiturates. On the basis of its interviews the commission calculated that 377,000 people in the state were depending on phenobarbital, Seconal, Tuinal, Amytal, and other such depressants of the central nervous system at least six times a month (which in this study was deemed to be "regular use.") These barbiturates, of course, are addictive when overused.

Nonbarbiturate sedatives were in use regularly by about 173,000—such products as Doriden, Noludar, etc. Addiction is possible.

Minor tranquilizers had 525,000 regular users. Some of the brand names: Librium, Valium, Atarax, Miltown, Equanil, Metprotabs, Lobritabel. With extremely high dosage and regular use, addiction is possible.

Major tranquilizers. Intended for psychotic patients,

these include such products as Stelazine and Mellaril and were used regularly by 85,000 seemingly normal people, the commission reported, to reduce panic, fear, hostility and agitation, and to "regularize thinking." There are so many unpleasant side effects that nonpsychotic users' addiction is unlikely.

Antidepressants, only 37,000 regulars. Brand names include Elavil, Tofranil, Marplan, etc. Addiction possibilities were undocumented.

Pep pills, the prescription amphetamines, dexedrine or benzedrine, had 110,000 regular users. Addiction is unlikely in pill form. But injection is another story, and even the pills can create psychological dependency.

Diet pills, 225,000 regulars. Most of these are amphetamine-like substances, sometimes combined with central nervous system depressants. Addiction is doubtful, but so is long-range effectiveness.

Controlled narcotics (nonheroin), 21,000 regulars. In this classification the natural narcotics include opium, the synthetics methadone. Addiction is a clear and present danger.

The illegal drugs:

Marijuana, 485,000 regulars.

LSD, 50,000 regulars (illegal except for federally approved research projects).

Methedrine, nicknamed "speed," 34,000 regulars. A highly potent stimulant of the central nervous system, taken intravenously to produce euphoria, it creates psychological dependency.

Heroin, 41,000 regulars. Very addictive, craved in constantly increasing doses.

Cocaine was not mentioned in the report, presumably because at that time it was little used. First known as a "social drug," it has proved to be highly antisocial, especially in the form of crack.

Drugs like LSD were used mostly by people in sales work, frequently while on the job. By contrast the most consistent customers for barbiturates and other sedatives, for antidepressants, minor tranquilizers, and diet pills were housewives. To nobody's surprise the occupational group which felt the least need for any of the drugs was farmers.

So our society, despite its Calvinist background, became a highly pilled one. Perhaps it was Mother's fault, for teaching us in childhood that taking medicine is a brave and moral thing to do. But the medical profession must share the blame: Faced with a patient eager for relief from the strains of daily life, many general practitioners fought down their reluctance and wrote out a prescription, because they feared if they did not, they might lose the patient to another doctor. Today, however, more and more doctors are sticking to their guns, and for several reasons.

One is that these pills never really solve anything, they only obscure it. Is it wise, for example, to make yourself feel secure when you're really in danger; or happy when you have reason to grieve; or full of energy when your body is fatigued and needs sleep? Aren't you more likely to correct a situation if you're disturbed by it? This is true not only of external problems—a bad job, or sexual troubles—but of strictly internal ones as well. A person overwhelmed by anxieties that have no discernible cause needs to get to a therapist of one kind or another. Tranquilizers may facilitate therapy, but if they prevent the person from embarking on it in the first place they are doing harm.

The other trouble with the mood pills is that even when they're not physically addictive, people become dependent on them if they take them for long. If pills help you through a specific crises, fine. But if you take them day in and day out for several years, you'll come to feel that you can't do without. Of course the same is true to some extent of any drug: some asthma patients cling to their medications even if their condition improves—though their breathing may be normal they will take a whiff from an inhalator any time they feel upset.

The most widely used drug of all in our society is alcohol, the foundation of an immense industry. It brings pleasure and relaxation when used carefully, and misery and destruction when yielded to.

Alcohol *is* a drug; its value as a food is almost nil. As with injected amphetamines, physical addiction is preceded by that easy psychological dependency. A drink before dinner is a reaction to stress, perhaps, but a pleasure reaction, even a benign one. Compulsive alcoholism is something else—a genuine stress disease that seriously damages the liver and the nervous system, sometimes fatally.

The drugs that improve your state of mind directly, without the diversions of alcohol—the taste, the thirst-gratification, the sociability—are more nakedly habit-forming. For this reason many doctors now refuse to prescribe such mood pills except in a temporary emergency, particularly for anyone under the magic age of thirty. As one medical man put it, "You should not start young people on these pills, but should seek other solutions to their problems. They're still flexible enough to do something about them. And there are physical dangers in a maintenance level of almost any medication over the years. Toxicity builds up. The patient will probably need increasing amounts of the drug, which in time means even more toxicity. Even a high level of aspirin intake can eventually produce a peptic ulcer."

Another reason many doctors are uneasy about writing prescriptions for psychotropic drugs—except in cases of clear-cut necessity—is that while they usually know the effects of any one drug on the average patient, they cannot always be sure what other drugs he may be taking at the same time, or what the resultant chemical interactions may do to his body. It is well known that barbiturates and alcohol together are far more potent than the sum of their separate effects. What about a patient under thyroid medication, who wakes up one morning and takes an energizer to recover from the phenobarbital that put him to sleep the night before, then goes to lunch with a friend, has a couple of martinis followed by two cups of black coffee, and proceeds to his dental appointment where he is given anesthesia so he can have a tooth pulled, followed by penicillin to prevent infection?

A team of physicians headed by Dr. Leighton E. Cluff performed a study in 1966 of the number of medications received by patients at Johns Hopkins, a first-rate hospital. Dr. Cluff's concern was adverse reactions to drugs, which are not infrequently lethal, and which he found rise rather spectacularly with the number of drugs given. Below is a chart showing how many patients received how many different drugs in the ordinary hospital routine, and what happened to them:

Drugs administered	Patients	Patients with bad reactions	Rate of bad reaction (%)
0–5	335	14	4.2
6–10	378	28	7.4
11–15	132	32	24.2
16–20	35	14	40.5
21 plus	20	9	45.0

One patient who had five different adverse reactions received thirty-seven different drugs.

Dr. Cluff's study, incidentally, did not include drugs taken *before* hospitalization, but at that time at Johns Hopkins, adverse drug reaction was the seventh most common cause for admission.

No consideration of pharmaceutical solutions to stress would be complete without a word about placebos—pills that contain no medication but that nevertheless work, because the patient believes they will work. All doctors know how effective they can be, and all doctors know that even "genuine" drugs are capable of curing people in part because of what is called the placebo effect.

Diphenylhydantion (DPH)—Delantin is the usual trade name—is not, by most standards, a placebo. It is a drug which was first used in 1937 to help epileptics. Apparently it has an inhibiting effect on the electrical storms which can sweep the brain, the current explanation for the common epileptic seizure, and it has proved invaluable in controlling that affliction. For a period of time, however, due to some degree to a philanthropist, DPH also came into usage for common stress.

Jack Dreyfus was the founder of one of Wall Street's most popular mutual funds. An acute, forceful man, the type who often seems to thrive on stress, he had ten years before begun to bend under his own force. His own description of his condition to Albert Rosenfield, science editor of *Life* magazine:

> I was anywhere from a little depressed to quite deeply depressed most of the time. There was an ever-present feeling of fear which varied in intensity during the day, and my mind was preoccupied with pessimistic and frequently angry thoughts. I had minor discomforts—chronic pains in the neck area and mild stomach upset. The happiest part of the day was the time when, with the help of sleeping medication, I was asleep. When I woke in the morning I was at my best. Usually around dusk, a little depressive cloud would descend on me and my hands and feet would get extremely cold.

Dreyfus was a man who did something about problems. After several physical examinations had revealed no cause for his distress, he sought help from the usual palette of pills: not only sedatives, but tranquilizers, mood elevators, and psychic energizers. None really helped. He also entered psychotherapy, but became preoccupied with the idea that his trouble was somehow electrical. He noticed a taste in his mouth resembling the flavor of ozone when he was depressed.

While talking with a neurologist he mentioned epilepsy and the doctor told him that the usual medication for that problem was DPH, because it turned down electrical effects in the brain. Dreyfus asked if he could try it. He got his prescription, and almost miraculously, within a few days, was cured. His aches and pains disappeared along with his depression. He gave up his psychiatrist, as well as all medication except for DPH. Subsequently Dreyfus set up a research foundation to investigate the nonepileptic uses of the drug.

The *Life* article stimulated immense interest in the public. Thousands wrote in for reprints and arranged to try DPH. In one case a man hunted up a doctor and got him to prescribe the drug, which was not difficult, because DPH has been proved over the years to have almost no side effects, and this man was for a number of reasons in rather haggard emotional shape. To his delight, DPH did for him exactly what it had done for Dreyfus. He began going about his life with satisfaction and zest, and for months it appeared that his problems were solved.

Then, suddenly, it stopped working—how or why the user could not say—but the clouds gathered once more and he began going downhill. Finally he had to seek out psychiatric counsel—and one of the first subjects he brought up was his mysterious trouble with DPH.

The doctor merely glanced at him and sighed. The Delantin, he explained, had probably had a placebo effect, and after a few months it had expired, as placebo effects so often do.

This patient was given some counseling, and over

the following months his state of mind gradually improved.

Bogus pills, or clinically inappropriate ones, are just the beginning of placebo medicine. Any treatment qualifies which has no definable curative powers but nevertheless improves the patient's health. This goes for the miracles at Lourdes and other examples of verified faith healing. Dr. William Menninger pointed out forty years ago that even conventional surgery can be an effective, if usually temporary, placebo, especially when, as so often is true, the surgeon has a compelling parental personality.

The best placebo of all in a way may well be that old doctor-patient relationship so dear to the American Medical Association. Dr. Albert Cornell, of New York, is a highly successful internist who credits many of his cures to what he simply calls education. After a thorough examination, he sits an ulcer patient, for example, in a comfortable chair and gives him a fifteen-minute illustrated lecture, beginning, "It isn't what you eat, but what eats you. Let me tell you about the vagus nerve, which is the brain's telephone line to the stomach. . . ." He explains how stress keeps the stomach working overtime until stomach acid finally penetrates the protective mucous membrane.

To the average doctor, fifteen minutes may sound like a lot of time to spend just talking, but if the patient's symptoms improve as a result, without medication, diet or surgery, it is fifteen minutes economically spent.

The same kind of treatment works on heart troubles too, on occasion. Here is a quite typical example. On the upper East Side of Manhattan, across the street from a great hospital, a doctor sat in his private office with a sheaf of laboratory reports and cardiograph tapes on the desk between him and a worried, middle-aged man whose heart for ten hours had been alternately leaping and skipping beats. The patient had returned the night before from an overworked, underslept business trip to California, jet-lagged. Arriving home, he found that a flood had left a foot of water in his suburban living room and inundated his basement tool room and wine cellar. He rushed out to buy a sump pump, then spent his evening trying to clean up the mess. In the middle of the night his heart had awakened him, going, "THUMP, thum, thumper . . . thump."

His local physician had wanted to put him into the hospital immediately, but this was a stubborn patient, who had experienced arrhythmia before. He accepted some medication, and made his way to the Manhattan practitioner who, he felt, knew more about his condition than any other medical man. This physician examined him thoroughly, sat him down across the desk full of test evidence, and began, "You're perfectly all right—nothing on the cardiogram, enzymes check out, no pain. It is simply that your heart signal is reeling." A half hour later the man, calm and reassured, was walking to Grand Central carrying his attache case like a thousand other businessmen on the avenue, his heart settled down to a steady, rhythmic beat. If your doctor can do this sort of thing for you, pay your bill promptly and cherish him.

This is not to say that most, or even many, disorders can be cured simply by talk, or that drugs, rest, diet and surgery, either singly or in combination, do not play an essential part in medical practice. Of course they do, but the physician is the person who must coordinate them all, and it is first necessary to understand the patient's true condition, which is seldom exclusively physical. Good doctors spend time on a diagnosis; they give unhurried attention to finding out what's really wrong, not simply what looks wrong at first glance, or what was wrong the last time. They then proceed to search through today's vast medical arsenal for those weapons that will do most to correct the problem, while causing minimal damage on the side. Among these weapons are both drugs and counseling, and a doctor who learns to use the two together is going to get better results.

One physician who spent years in general practice, Dr. William J. Goldwag, says: "It is an accepted fact that eighty-five percent of the ailments brought to a general practitioner will get better and five percent will get worse regardless of what the doctor does. The remaining ten percent is where the doctor makes a difference. But if the doctor is under so much pressure that he cannot give each patient a decent attention span, they may all get worse."

The fact that so many general physicians are so stress-ridden themselves (heart attacks are commoner in doctors than in almost any other professional group) may be the reason many of their patients are turning to less conventional methods of stress relief.

SUPPORT GROUPS

It was on their own initiative, and largely without medical advice, that Americans in the 1960s began flocking into encounter and sensitivity groups, which turned classical psychotherapy inside out in marathon meetings aimed at achieving the quick, sudden—and often explosively emotional—opening up of previously guarded personalities. Encounter groups have been described as treatment for people who are not sick but who are simply seeking fulfillment. Nevertheless, their aims were decidedly therapeutic—to make individuals feel human again, at ease with their own emotions and those of the people around them, despite the depersonalizing industrial society in which we live. The encounter groups constituted a kind of mass folk therapy, and it is estimated that some two million Americans were moved to join in.

The National Training Laboratories are generally credited with having started the movement, when they began organizing T (for Training) groups for corporation employees shortly after World War II, but the roots go back much farther. It was just after the turn of this century that a Boston doctor named J. H. Pratt began holding classes for tubercular patients who could not afford to go away to a mountain sanitarium, the preferred treatment for TB at the time. Pratt's initial purpose was a modest one: to teach his patients to care for themselves at home—what to eat, how much to rest, how to keep temperature charts, etc. Inevitably, however, the patients raised questions dealing with emotional problems, and the discussions which followed seemed to benefit them both mentally and physically.

It all worked very well, and the camaraderie among the patients in the classes seemed to be part of the reason. Dr. Pratt kept at it for fifty years, and by the middle of the century was referring to the classes frankly as group psychotherapy. Meanwhile in Europe, as early as 1910, Dr. J. L. Moreno, a Viennese psychiatrist, had also begun to deal with patients in groups, and had evolved a technique called psychodrama, the acting out of neuroses in order to dispel them.

Group psychiatry received a big boost as an approved medical method during World War II, when it came into extensive use in the U.S. Army. Then, in the years just after the war the psychologists began to evolve the encounter groups, and the road forked. Group therapy went one way, and the encounter movement went the other.

The early encounter groups often specialized in specific problems. There is stress to a corporate merger situation, there is stress to a bad marriage—or sometimes to a good one for that matter—and in a sophisticated community you might find a different group focusing on each of these areas. The NTL got its start specializing in the problems of specific employee groups in the big corporations—treasurers, controllers, presidents, general executives, and also workers in almost any rank who felt trapped in a cocoon of ineffectiveness. From the seeds of NTL sprang movements like Esalen, based in California, which went into hairier personal relationships.

The typical encounter group often started out very cautiously, even timidly, until some organizing type—sometimes the leader, sometimes a bold member—decided to propose a set of aims and procedures. When this happened, some of the others might start protesting, and the game was on. Soon everyone was working on everyone else, often first in anger, but gradually affection and many other emotions began to emerge. The participants might never see one another outside the group (some used only first names), so they felt they might as well let go and discover something. Masks disappeared. It was the opposite of the usual cocktail party chatter.

One of the core groups was The Center for Studies of the Person in La Jolla, California, the base of the late Carl Rogers, who was generally regarded as the philosopher of the movement. Rogers wrote:

> What is the psychological need that draws people into encounter groups? I believe it is a hunger for something the person does not find in his work environment, in his church, certainly not in his school or college, and sadly enough, not even in modern family life. It is a hunger for relationships which are close and real; in which feelings and emotions can be spontaneously expressed without first being carefully censored or bottled up; where deep experiences—disappointments and joys—can be shared; where new ways of behaving can be risked and tried out; where, in a word, he approaches the state where all is known

and accepted, and thus further growth becomes possible. . . .

In a group, facades are cracked open and light is let in . . . people get taken back into the human race. . . .*

In time, however, the encounter movement peaked. The intellectual vanguard who had pursued it first became a little bored perhaps, and, for certain, all the respectable professionals became concerned about the lurid publicity that the more radical groups engendered. It had become a great field for irresponsible promoters looking to become gurus.

Today the encounter movement has largely given way to support groups, going back to the original Pratt method in which people with similar problems meet together every week or so to share their pain and look for ways of coping with it. The atmosphere is sympathetic rather than confrontational. There are support groups for people whose spouses have recently died; there are support groups for people who want to stop smoking but haven't been able to do it alone. And there is the overwhelming spiritual alchemy of Alcoholics Anonymous, a group of long standing that is broadly acknowledged to have accomplished more cures of its particular stress syndrome than any religious, pharamacological, or even strictly psychiatric approach.

MEDITATION

Another practice widely used for stress is meditation of one sort or another. The basic methods are derived from yoga and Zen; their purpose is to achieve calm contemplation of the self in the cosmos, sometimes

*Carl R. Rogers, *Carl Rogers on Encounter Groups*, Harper & Row, 1970.

tied to mild physical exercise. Meditation is a surprising technique to be seized on by a country as proudly pragmatic as ours, but some of the most skeptical of middle-aged Americans who try it insist that this is the best buffer of all against the illnesses due to stress.

It first caught on in this country with what was called Transcendental Meditation. Many Americans first heard of TM in 1967, when the Beatles and Mia Farrow tripped off to the Himalayas to learn about it from Maharishi Mahesh Yogi, a colorful monk with a gift for offhand organizing and a genius for attracting glowing, well-educated young advocates. The Maharishi took a university degree in physics himself, spent thirteen years studying the ancient Vedic tradition of India with a scholarly guru, and then retreated to a monastery for two years. He emerged with a benign, but busy, determination to convert the world not to his religion but to a secular method of achieving inner tranquility.

As early as 1965 the Maharishi had narrowed his sights on North America as the most fertile ground for his ideas; he concentrated on gathering and training teachers, who in turn spread the gospel to others until the number of meditators in the United States alone reached an estimated million. The early apostles of TM in the United States traveled with rock groups in order to find an audience; but later ones mostly delivered their lectures before civic clubs and in suburban public libraries. They made it a point to wear reasonable haircuts, neckties and jackets, and many of them were both dedicated and disarmingly skilled as teachers. After two evening lectures, the TM initiate would receive a session of individual instruction. He learned to sit down and close his eyes for two periods of twenty minutes each day, during which time he, in effect, vacated the stress battlefield, willing himself into a state called "restful alertness." He did this by concentrating on the silent repetition of a word called a mantra, a soothing, meaningless sound, secretly assigned by the instructor in an initiation ceremony.

Whether because of the mantra or not, most beginners learned quite readily how to ease off into quietude. Their hands and feet felt heavy and tingling and their minds idle. Thoughts floated. The Maharishi obviously recognized that the nature of American life would make meditation of Oriental intensity and duration—the kind he himself practiced as a monk—inappropriate for mass use here (perhaps even slightly risky). But done twice a day for just twenty minutes each time, the TM prescription was extremely soothing.

The initiation did not complete the course. The learner later attended three successive question-and-answer meetings with twenty to thirty other new initiates. Here he learned of some surprising problems in meditation, because first reactions to TM vary widely. The biggest change in the author after he began meditating was a marked increase in the number of dreams during sleep. But some novices reported that they wept or had headaches at first, and some noticed that pet animals seemed to be strangely attracted to them. What do you do about an Afghan hound who wants to sit in your lap while you're reading the newspaper? After discussing difficulties such as these, the meeting culminated in a period of group meditation, and then everyone went home (though one or two might linger to ask the instructor a more private question: What was that mantra of mine again?).

It wasn't long before TM caught the fascinated attention not only of psychologists but of certain researchers in physiology as well. Dr. Herbert Benson, a cardiologist at Harvard Medical School, began using transcendental meditators as test subjects, and he became convinced that the technique lowered their likelihood of contracting some common stress disorders. Working with physiologist Robert Keith Wallace, Benson established that in meditation there is marked reduction of oxygen consumption, the prime measure of metabolic rate. The reduction, he pointed out, is greater than after six hours of sleep. The arterial concentration of lactate, a chemical sometimes correlated with anxiety, dropped four times faster in meditation than in simple rest. Galvanic skin resistance, another positive key to relaxation, in some cases increased fourfold. On the basis of his data he endorsed meditation as a medical technique for treating the twenty two million Americans who suffer from high blood pressure.

Does meditation help with the ordinary stresses of life? At the height of its popularity, thousands swore it did, including a substantial number of high school students who decided they preferred it to marijuana. One middle-aged Chicago automobile salesman, a skeptic who finally tried meditation at the urging of his daughter, reported wonderingly: "I not only get along better with people—and with myself—I'm more effective on the job. This thing is useful." The timing, incidentally, is very apt for suburban commuters. That man sitting opposite you in the train may have his eyes closed not in sleep, but in restful meditation, getting over his day at the office.

In the big-city phonebooks, listings for classes in yoga and other Oriental disciplines abound, most of them much more deeply drawn, more intricate, and more demanding than ordinary meditation. Sometimes the teacher is also something of a priestly leader, a guru, a person of intense charisma. The most famous of these in this century and the man who may have set the pattern was the late G. I. Gurdjieff, whose philosophical-ethical-mystical-physical movement of the 1920s in Europe has survived him.

In these movements derived from the East, diet is often involved, with vegetarian emphasis and much of the Oriental staple, brown rice, as in macrobiotics. Almost always there is also a degree of deliberate detachment from the turmoil of daily urban life, and surrender to a group. The erasure of ego can produce a semi-monkish calm and ease many stresses in living. The religious aura puts many people off, but the religiousness is often more by inference than actuality once these movements are transported West. What godliness survives is benign rather than specific—an inward Eastern intuitiveness as compared with Western moral logic.

This is not true of all the Eastern movements, of course; some sects demand surrender of all liberty and worldly goods, as in Hare Krishna, turning their members into fervid missionaries.

In all of these mystical and semi-mystical approaches, as well as in the recent growth of pentecostal religion, and in the support groups too, for that matter—much of the point for today's practitioners lies in developing self-awareness—with an emphasis on the whole self, as distinguished from the rational, ego-centered fragment-of-self so prominently featured in conventional Western culture. The human personality, these people assert, is not simply a machine for efficient living, and its methods are not purely mechanical. People possess feelings and capacities outside the realm of the intellect, or even the conventional drives, often irrational, often of no practical use, which however need to be expressed and exercised, or the person is not fully human. We need to dream at night, whether or not we remember the dream the next morning; it has been demonstrated that people who do not dream enough become tense and anxious. Night dreams, daydreams, fantasy, trances more or less hypnotic, hallucinations mild and strong, all are forms of consciousness expansion and all are natural and enriching functions of the human mind, according to these proponents.

Dr. Andrew Weill believes that this hunger for irrational inner experience is the real reason behind the rise in drug consumption: drugs (including alcohol) do alter consciousness without effort or training, and thus fill a need that Western civilization cannot fill otherwise—indeed, does not even recognize. Weill points out that many people lose interest in drugs when they take up meditation—because, he says, meditation fills this same need, only better.

The self-awareness movements wax and wane, and are identified by many names. One called Arica came on strong in New York, San Francisco, Boston, Miami, San Diego, Pittsburgh, and Los Angeles. It was originated by a Brazilian named Oscar Ichazo in 1970, after he had spent years studying esoteric practices in South America, China, Afghanistan, and Tibet. Ichazo claimed to have selected the most effective practices of various cults and put them together—the name Arica came from the town in Chile where a group of about fifty people, many from the United States, spent ten months as Ichazo's first students. Arica takes much time and effort; the intensive course lasts six weeks, ten hours a day.

I once visited Arica. Its Manhattan headquarters at that time was off Fifth Avenue just below Central Park, a neighborhood of expensive specialty shops such as Bergdorf Goodman, Bonwit Teller, and Henri Bendel. Outside, numerous stylish people trod the sidewalks, most of them discreetly hostile or, at best, carefully indifferent. But within Arica the faces were different. As you walked down a corridor, you suddenly discovered that someone coming the other way was studying your eyes with interest, and his mouth wore a quiet smile. In the middle of New York, the most impersonal city in the world, a total stranger was looking into your face trustfully. It was almost unnerving. A zombie quality? Perhaps a little, but the genuine zombies were downstairs, walking confidently up and down the sidewalks.

BIOLOGICAL FEEDBACK

The public grabs so fast at anything claiming to relieve stress that biofeedback became an in word before most people knew what it meant. Yet biological feedback research is among the most promising, if technically intricate, of therapeutic methods now being developed in the stress field. Much of the laboratory expense for this development has been paid for by the Pentagon, eager to learn anything that may help servicemen withstand the specialized stresses of combat or imprisonment.

Behind biofeedback lies something of a revolution in medical theory. People's skeletal muscles are obviously at the command of their will. You can force your arms to move up and down, your eyelids to blink fast or slow. But it has been postulated until recently that people cannot consciously control their autonomic nervous system, the unseen regulator of such processes as pulse rate, glandular secretion, and oxygen consumption—the complex mechanisms which, when they go wrong, so frequently trigger the stress diseases.

Dr. Neal E. Miller of Rockefeller University challenged this assumption several decades ago with the then outrageous hypothesis that laboratory animals might be taught to control their autonomic systems through a schedule of rewards and punishments. He and his associate, Leo V. Di Cara, then at Yale's Medical School, drugged rats with curare to put their skeletal-muscular systems out of action, and then used electric shock as a teaching tool. Soon they had revised medical dogma. The rats could indeed be taught to control interior processes. In one of Miller's most famous exploits, one rat was regularly induced to send enough blood to one ear to make it blush, while the other ear blanched. Miller is a scientist, cautious about drawing deductions, but he admitted several years ago that he thought that human beings, in this respect, were probably as smart as rats. He and a number of other scattered medical researchers have set about to prove it.

Taking advantage of the many delicate electronic devices available today, medical doctors and psychologists have set up systems in which patients or study subjects are kept continuously informed of what is going on within certain organs. For example, a tiny sensor is swallowed by a subject trying to control the acid in his stomach. When the acid becomes excessive—perhaps copious enough to burn a hole in the stomach membrane—the sensor registers this fact on a meter in front of the subject. After a time, by concentrating on the meter's signal, the subject may learn to moderate the flow. Nobody yet knows just how one does this, and the theories are abstruse. But the feedback signal is the vital element, the tool by which one learns. And having learned, you can sometimes then go out into the stressful world and control your visceral response without needing the visible feedback signal any longer.

The most dramatic demonstration of feedback benefits to date involves the heart. With two or three days of training, subjects can be taught to slow their heartbeats. Subtle errors in rhythm can also be adjusted. At the Gerontology Research Center of the National Institute of Child Health and Human Development in Baltimore, five out of eight cardiac patients were taught by psychologist Bernard Engel and Dr. Theodore Weiss to correct premature ventricular contraction, a dangerous arrhythmia, by biofeedback. Other biofeedback experts have been able to train hypertense people to lower their systolic readings.

One of the most effective uses of biofeedback is in treating migraine. These terrible headaches are caused by dilation in the arteries of the head and scalp, and they can be mitigated or avoided, two Menninger Foundation doctors discovered, by teaching patients to raise their hand temperatures as much as twenty-five degrees by dilating the hand arteries. When this happens, the arteries in the head contract as a physical corollary, heading off the migraine. The surprising thing is how easy it is to get the knack of willing the hands warmer, simply by recalling other times when they were warm because of the sun, or an open wood fire, or even under a hot-air hand drier in a restaurant washroom. Eighty percent of the patients studied at the Menninger Foundation were helped by the technique, which is now being recommended by many headache specialists.

At the University of Colorado Medical School Dr. Johann Stoyva and Dr. Thomas Budzynski devised a similar method for treating those headaches caused by muscular tension, another very common stress symptom, although not attributable to the autonomic nervous system. Using an electromyograph to measure contractions in the muscles of the forehead, they could train subjects to ease their tension—and their headaches—by scoring against a feedback signal. This technique, once learned, can bring relief to insomniacs as well.

Among the more intriguing of the biofeedback techniques have been those developed for the brain itself. In the 1920s, Hans Berger of the University of Jena in Germany established that the brain emits different electrical signals during different activities. The brain gives off the highest frequency signal when it is under pressure to complete tasks; this signal is called beta. Next down the scale is alpha, reflecting a more relaxed and contemplative mood. Then comes theta, associated with creative thinking; and delta, the lowest frequency, which comes with sleep. An electroencephalograph is used to monitor the activity within the brain.

It has been demonstrated conclusively that people can be trained through feedback to shift their brains from beta to alpha and sometimes even to theta. The trainee is installed in a quiet room and fitted with two electrodes to the scalp plus a ground wire attached to an ear. At his feet is an electrical indicator that will register the total alpha-wave score he has achieved during each one- or two-minute interval of drilling. During the attempt, his success—or lack of it—will be made evident to him by means of a tone that swells in amplitude when the brain switches to alpha. After the training session, he can also, with technical help, trace the pattern on the read-out from the EEG machine.

No instructions on how to go about achieving alpha are given. The reason is that directions might make the subject too dependent on the director, and the objective is to train him so that he eventually can summon alpha without using the machine.

While wired, most people begin to find their way into alpha through introspection, summoning up particularly peaceful moments from their past. One subject may recall a lyrical day in a sailboat, or dancing—though he may not have danced, or thought about it, in years. Moments with young children are another staple, as are recollections of sensual repose.

The first hour of striving for alpha, while pleasant in many ways, can be surprisingly tiring. But by the time the second session comes up, trainees discover they have already made some progress. Their thoughts become less specific, as the inventory of memory is exhausted, and the alpha state becomes more trance-like and self-sustaining, attuned to the signal alone. Their scores rise. Almost anyone can learn to attain consistent A, though it may take as many as ten hours of training.

There is an obvious connection between the attainment of alpha on EEG feedback and the various forms of meditation, but no feedback student has yet succeeded in matching the accomplishments of Eastern mystics. Yoga and Zen masters wired to the EEG and other testing machines have demonstrated extraordinary control of autonomic functions—using very little oxygen, not reacting to pain, and registering theta, or in some cases delta, although they remain completely aware of what is going on around them. Even in the Orient, however, relatively few people meditate as a regular practice, and only a handful are masters.

One expert who has tried both meditation and feedback and written papers on them is Durand Kiefer. He began his research in 1959 and traveled widely for ten years to study various disciplines. He concluded that the best solution is a combination of meditation and feedback. The most demanding pure meditation regimen he experienced came during his nine months as a student at Zenshinji monastery at Tassajara in Japan, where he practiced Zen Buddhist *zazen,* sometimes for as long as twelve hours a day; he achieved stressless bliss for a few moments at a time, he reported in a talk to the Bio-feedback Research Society, but it was very slow work. By contrast, he wrote, "Every hour spent in meditation with EEG alpha feedback has produced some degree of euphoria—the sense of well-being and general serenity of the sort called grace in the Christian terminology. Perhaps within another decade the number of alpha masters, theta masters, and delta masters living among us may exceed the number of Zen masters, yoga masters, and Sufi masters who have lived since time began."

On the other side of the fence is Dr. Bernard Glueck, director of research at the Institute of Living, in Hartford. His research indicated to him that although biofeedback does produce alpha, even the easiest meditation techniques do it better because they synchronize all parts of the brain. Glueck told a round table on the subject of anxiety that, when an experienced meditator begins using his mantra, "it's literally like turning a switch in the brain." He added, "Maybe there is another window into the unconscious. Dreams are one; this could be a second."

HYPNOSIS

Another argument about alpha waves—whether meditation-produced or machine-made—relates to the part self-hypnosis may play in the process. Some meditators and feedback advocates rear back at the notion, but medical scientists, when pressed, are less negative. Hypnosis, after numberless excursions into the carnival world, has come quietly back to respectability in science. It is used for surgical anethesia as well as in day-to-day dentistry. Techniques for painless childbirth, whatever their proponents may claim, are essentially hypnotic. More significantly, people can be cured of warts by hypnosis and of certain more serious afflictions, implying an actual change in their immunological responses. And there is little doubt in the minds of some American doctors currently studying the Chinese technique of acupuncture that hypnosis does much of the job there too, although there appear to be neural pathways involved as well. As with hypnosis, not all patients take well to acupuncture, even on mainland China.

Dr. Herbert Spiegel, a New York psychiatrist who teaches at Columbia University's College of Physicians and Surgeons, is an outstanding—and most reputable—expert on hypnosis. After using it to cure an attack of asthma, for example, he trains the patient to maintain the cure by self-hypnosis, as follows: "Roll your eyes upward, close them, take a deep breath. Let your clenched hand float upward. Imagine your bronchii opening. Tell yourself they will stay open when your eyes are open. Open your fist slowly and then your eyes.'' Certainly it sounds not unlike meditation and biofeedback, and Spiegel himself agrees. He says: "Whether you attach electrodes to your head or listen to a priest in a saffron robe, it is all essentially the same. Call it Zen, acupuncture, meditation, biofeedback, or Mesmer, it taps the same kind of attentive, narrowed inner concentration, erasing peripheral distractions—and it can be very useful.''

Even the newest treatments for stress may not be so very new in essence. Practicing Quakers say that the essential part of their meetings is not the arousal of some member to ''speak'' but the inward contemplation by the whole congregation in a plain, placid place. "Centering down," a prominent term in the jargon of awareness groups, is an old Quaker expression. Christian Science fights disease with inward spiritual peace. Even in the Roman Catholic Church the chants, the repetition of the rosary, the saying of the Office, may have a hypnotic effect, and there is some disagreement on the effectiveness of a high mass as delivered in the new English version, compared with the ancient, and more mysteriously moving, Latin.

In 1972 the National Institute of Mental Health set up a program in which interested modern-day Navajos were paid to apprentice themselves to traditional tribal medicine men on the Arizona reservation. They learned the rituals, the sand drawings, the herbs, chants, and dances used over the centuries to treat the sick. As an approving student put it: ''Navajo doctors are completely different from white anglo doctors. You go to a hospital and maybe once a day the doctor comes around and he stays there maybe five minutes. About the only thing they do is put something in your mouth and see how hot you are. The rest of the time you just lie there. But the medicine men help you all the time—they give you lots of medicine and they sing all night.''

It is easy to dismiss some of the techniques described in this chapter as esoteric entertainments, of little practical value. But there is an important shared significance—perhaps a revolutionary one—in all of them, including also exercise and diet. They all depend on the active participation of the patient. That is part of their appeal, as well as one of the reasons why they are effective.

One more thing must be emphasized: None of these therapies is intended to replace traditional nuts-and-bolts medical care. They work as adjuncts, not substitutes, and before undertaking any of them you should get a complete physical examination from your doctor. Should he find some specific medical condition that interferes with your plan, you will have to make changes. If his objections are only general, on the other hand, listen to him, but if you're not convinced, seek out another physician who may be more open-minded. Whatever you do, however, don't undertake a program without competent medical approval based on a detailed knowledge of your individual state of health.

Assuming no obstacles arise, what form of therapy should you turn to?

This has to depend on what kind of person you find yourself to be, perhaps by trying several diverse approaches. One kind of person cannot be hypnotized by even the most skilled practitioner, while another is highly hypnotizable.* People with a moderately strong

*Dr. Spiegel grades capacity to be hypnotized from zero to five. *Zero* includes schizophrenics, psychopaths and mental defectives who, he says, cannot be hypnotized. Another *zero* group are those who have no biological capacity for hypnosis but are mentally sound. At the other end of

dependent streak take well to psychotherapy, especially if they can speak their feelings fairly easily. A specific coronary patient, on the other hand, may be too impatient for the turgid processes of a psychiatrist's office; he might be better off on a feedback machine, where he is his own boss, aiming toward clear-cut, practical goals that he can understand.

What method of treatment you choose depends also on what you are suffering from. If your condition is a specific physical one—asthma, or arrhythmia, say—a highly specific technique, such as feedback or hypnosis, may be the answer. Meditation, on the other hand, aims at improving one's state of mind, and/or way of life, and the physiological side effects, though demonstrable, are more or less incidental. Psychotherapy can go either way.

Then there is the matter of money. Most of us cannot afford psychoanalysis,† and even the relatively short-term forms of therapy commonly used in treating psychosomatic illnesses can be painful to pay for. But when they work they are often economical in the long run, if the condition would otherwise become a chronic one.

How do you go about locating a reputable hypnotist, or a biofeedback center, or a good support group? Your doctor may be able to help. If not, another approach is to seek out a professional in your town, one who has been there for a period of years and is thoroughly

the scale are the *fives*, "imaginative, tactile, intuitive people, often scientists, musicians or artists, with little time sense" who take very easily to hypnosis. Less appropriate candidates for hypnosis are those classified as *one*, described by Spiegel as "analytical people, linear thinkers." However, these, and others low on the numbering scale, often may respond well to psychoanalysis, whereas people on the high end of the scale may be so trance prone that if they enter analysis they may actually contract additional neurotic symptoms, by suggestion, if the analyst is not aware of their unique sensitivity.

† Freud charged $8.10 a session fifty years ago, but today the going rate is $75 to $150—between $54,000 and $108,000 for a three-year, five-day-a-week treatment.

acquainted with the community's resources. Depending on what you are after, this person might be a psychologist, a general practitioner, a member of the clergy, or the employee of a social service agency. Explain that what you want at the moment is not treatment but advice, and listen carefully to what he or she tells you. In the end, you may find yourself following several of these paths and getting help from all of them, at least for a time.

But there is something important to understand.

One of the puzzling truths about medical treatment in general—particularly treatment for stress conditions—is the way it often succeeds at first, and then later gradually fails. "Placebo effect" does not altogether explain this pheonomenon, for it occurs with drugs that have clearly demonstrable physical effects, and it occurs with surgery. It particularly occurs with shock treatment for psychotic mental patients. Even today no one knows just how shock treatment works, only that when it does, it makes patients feel dramatically better, and that its effects usually run out after a year or two.

Shock treatment can be administered either electrically or chemically (by the intravenous injection of Metrazol or, more rarely, insulin), and it is generally assumed to stimulate a rallying of the patient's resources analogous to the immune response upon the onset of infection. Another less drastic therapy involving shock is the intravenous injection of acetylcholine, which causes a short period of cardiac arrest—a half-minute or so—and unconsciousness.

Seemingly the opposite of shock is sleep treatment, practiced in Europe to treat emotionally disturbed people, putting them away, back in the cradle, so to speak, for a week or so, out of the adult world. The technique utilized can be either chemical or electrical although there is some danger of pneumonia in both procedures. There are also two other well-known European methods of treating the stressed, both of them inexplicable medically and both barred in the United States. The first is the injection program at the famous Dr. Ana Aslan's Geriatric Institute of Bucharest, Rumania; her substance is called Gerovital, and is principally novocaine. The other is cellular transplants, originated by a Swiss surgeon, the late Dr. Paul Niehans. In 1927, treating a young human dwarf, Niehans tried intramuscular injection of a pulp made from the pituitary cells of a fetal calf, with, he reported, excellent results in stimulating growth. In subsequent years he developed an entire palette of cell-types, for the treatment of various human afflictions.

Some doubters—and the majority of physicians falls into the category—propose that if cellular therapy does work it probably does so, again, by administering shock to the human system, stimulating natural rallying. The dangers are numerous, including incalculable allergic responses; medical proof of the merits of the treatment is lacking, apart from empirical reports; and the technique has been callously exploited in some of the places where it is permitted legally. Yet many people hold that they have been helped by it.

The truth is that shock of some sort is probably a basic ingredient of all medical treatment, from pills to surgery to psychotherapy to "rest cures," as well as in such body-conditioning practices as the sauna, in which you spend an hour in an extremely hot, dry room and then immediately plunge into an icy pool. Challenge the body: change its pace: shake it up: free it of the old patterns: get it moving again, naturally and spontaneously.

A century ago people often found cures for a medical condition in travel, or in religion, or even in love— Elizabeth Barrett was a bed-ridden invalid until she met Robert Browning. From our modern scientific eminence we smile at those Victorians. But theirs were remedies that actually worked, at least for many sufferers, at least for a while. They worked in part through belief—the placebo effect—but probably they also worked in part through shock—the shock of a sudden change in the patient's situation. And both faith and shock remain important curative forces in the practice of medicine today.

Shock, however, is by nature temporary. Gradually its effects fade; normality of some sort—or what we think of as normality—ensues; the old responses to stress start building into patterns again, patterns that are both mental and physiological. And when they build far enough, the symptoms begin sprouting once more.

The fact that one or another of these regimens fades in its effectiveness for you six months after you undertake it is not unusual, and should not discourage you. Get deeper into it. Don't allow it to become simply another routine. If, after persistence, it cannot help you, try another. The fight against stress is not a single battle but a very long war of survival, and many campaigns may be necessary.

There are also ways of understanding, and perhaps thus altering, the stressors themselves, the external conditions under which we live, and that is what the final chapter of this book is about.

CHAPTER 10

Stress and the Drive for Success

In a thirteenth-century document called *The King's Mirror*, an anonymous Norwegian writer asked himself why certain of his countrymen were willing to undergo the hard, dangerous sea voyage to settle Greenland, and he found the answer in what he called the three-fold character of human nature:

> One part thereof is the spirit of rivalry and craving for fame. . . . The second is the thirst for knowledge. . . . The third thing is the hope of wealth; for men look to that wherever they learn that a gain can be expected, regardless that great dangers threaten them on the other side.

In *Tender Is the Night*, F. Scott Fitzgerald wrote of his hero, Dick Diver:

> He wanted to be good, he wanted to be brave and wise . . . he wanted to be loved, too, if he could fit that in.

A smoldering hope pervades human life. We set up objectives for this hope—money, knowledge, love, recognition, virtue. But what we are really yearning after is something larger: the feeling that we matter; that we make a difference. We must say something with our lives, and what we say must be heard—by history if at all possible; if not, then by our contemporaries, many or few; and if they won't listen we turn toward God. Hope inclines us to believe in God, or something like God.

Despair inclines us to disbelieve, and is the darker force that also drives us, side by side with the bright force of hope. We fight despair. We run from it. We try to bury it in dark corners. We rush around and make a commotion to drown out its desolating monotone. But we can never get rid of it for good, this feeling that life is an empty ocean, and we are bubbles that form, and float for a while, and then disappear, and that's all there is: we were made to be destroyed.

Fitzgerald himself felt all this acutely, and at the age of thirty-nine went through a crisis that he later called "The Crack-Up," something wider than emotional or physical breakdown but including both, a breakdown in his life itself. He had gotten what he wanted, and had dropped and broken it. He had had the chance and had wasted it. Success had failed him. He had failed success. He had failed his life.

With time Fitzgerald recovered. He stopped drinking, and began writing again. But he no longer worried about being brave, or wise or good. Perhaps he was like Dr. LeShan's cancer patient who said, "Last time I hoped and look what happened. . . . I'll never hope again." Five years after "The Crack-Up" Fitzgerald, forty-four years old, died of a heart attack.

Hope and despair propel people along a course that often veers sharply from one side of the road to the other. The boss raises your salary: suddenly you matter. He lets you go: suddenly you don't. Your lover leaves you for someone else: you don't. *You* fall in love with someone else: you do again. Your daughter wins a scholarship: and you both matter. In this way people go through life scoring themselves, and though they sometimes pretend otherwise these scores matter intensely. They also put us under great strain. One practicing psychiatrist was asked what single medicine would most help his average patient, all things possible: self-insight?

better relations with the family? The psychiatrist thought for a moment. Then he sighed. Then he smiled—a little ruefully. "Success," he answered at last. "A little ordinary, worldly success."

Another gave the same kind of smile but was even more specific. His answer: "Money."

Money is only one mark of success in our time and place, but it is a specific one, a hard-edged worldly one, and in its way quite a rational one, and it is what much of our society's struggle revolves around daily. You can count money up. You can hold it in your hand. You can exchange it for something that you value. You can set it aside for a rainy day. You can't do these things with love or with fame, and you can only do some of them with power.

Rich people aren't always happy, but most of them possess quite well-developed egos—a knowledge that they are of importance. They are of importance in the world. They are of importance in their families, where they often remain central figures into old age and even senility.

Money also frees, at least it is capable of freeing. Admittedly, not everyone knows what to do with the freedom: How do you spend your life if you don't have to spend it earning a living? Some decide to spend it that way anyway, and turn into compulsive money-makers, millionaires in constant tension over where their next million is coming from, as enslaved by wealth as poor people are by their lack of it. Money can confuse people; it can make problems.

But it can solve them, too.

Say that you lose your job. This is a demoralizing experience for rich and poor alike. But if you're poor you must scramble. You've got to find work right away, never mind if it suits your temperament, and even if it means a cut in salary. If you search your soul at all it is to conclude that you'd better keep your mouth shut from now on, and also learn to get up on time in the morning. But if you're someone with an income, you have time. You can shop around. You can take people out to lunch and find out where the opportunities lie. You can travel to distant cities. And you can take a month or two to think things out. Maybe your heart isn't really in advertising, and you decide to go back to college again and train to become a teacher. Thus you change your career and your life. All this you can do because you have money.

There are other ways people assert their value in the world, if none are quite so negotiable as money. One of these is recognition: the name in the newspaper, the prize won, the election to the PTA board, or the union office, or even to government. The jobs are worth doing in themselves but often their greatest personal importance is as badges of success pinned on us by judges around us. It is almost pathetic how much the smallest gestures of society, the minor little honors, can mean to people, even when they convey nothing tangible. When we are in school we wonder why in the name of sanity people run for the student council. Later in life we understand it better. Being smiled upon by our peers, or even voted for, feels very good.

One night I was mayor of New York City—or night mayor, more precisely. Mayor John Lindsay, to make sure someone was always on hand to deal with the problems of anxious citizens, had recruited an after-hours corps of young telephone answerers, and he asked various members of his administration to take turns sitting in an office all night to deal with the more perplexing calls. As a member of the City Planning Commission, I showed up at City Hall on New Year's Eve of 1971.

It was an icy night, and while there were a few disasters and major tragedies reported, most of the calls were from tenants in apartment buildings which had no heat, hardly a minor matter in that weather. What my crew at the switchboard did was to ascertain, if possible, the name of the building's owner or manager and then phone him directly, routing him out of bed if necessary. Conversations to landlords at two in the morning beginning, "This is the Mayor's office . . ." sometimes, but not always, got warming results. If not, follow-up action was arranged for the morrow from city staff people.

When the phone was not ringing, I had time to wander around my office. It was not the mayor's official office, but was on the floor just below, a large room about twenty-five by seventeen feet, and if not shabby, quite worn. In the center was a convertible couch made up with blankets labeled "Kings County Medical Center, Department of Hospitals, NYC." The pillowcase was stamped "Bellevue Hospital, Staff Adm.," as was the towel in the bathroom. There were four blazing fluorescent ceiling lights of the type common to schoolrooms, and a battered TV set. The room had been used by the mayor's immediate predecessor as a makeshift gymnasium during his tenure; beside the shower in the bathroom was not only an old scale for weighing oneself, but a unicycle leaning forlornly against the wall, with a flat tire, long out of office.

But in the main the contents of the office were souvenirs of success.

There were a dozen or so medals, including several B'nai B'rith awards, and the Sovereign Greek Order of St. Denis of Zante. There were numerous photographs, ranging from a signed portrait of David Ben-Gurion to a photo of JVL riding a bicycle six feet high labeled "Things to do in the Spring." Also a picture of the ground-breaking at the New York Civic Center Campus, with Mayor Lindsay not just smiling his usual fine smile, but laughing outright. At a meeting I attended later, that multi-million-dollar project was dropped from the capital budget.

But above all, there were the plaques from civic organizations: thirty-eight of them hanging on the walls, and another twenty or so propped up at floor level waiting to be elevated. Here are a few samples, jotted down in my middle-of-the-night inventory:

Manhattan Kiwanis Foundation Man of the Year, December 1964: John V. Lindsay, Congressman 17th District, for his effort on behalf of underprivileged children.

Sanitation Department of the City of New York: Sanitation man (honorary) first class (detached to sweeping duties at City Hall) 23 August, 1966.

The Assembly of Captive European Nations Award: Their Tenth Anniversary Commemorative Medal to the Honorable John V. Lindsay, September 20, 1964.

New York Yankees cordially extend all privileges of Yankee Stadium to the Hon. John V. Lindsay, signed, Dan Topping.

NAER TORMID SOCIETY (honorary member), Fire Department, City of New York, 3 November 1965.

Young Republicans Club, 1966.

Odd Fellows Welfare Club.

Greater New York Council Boy Scouts of America, in appreciation, Financial Dinnerama, January 20, 1966.

There was also a mounted deer head. Hanging on the rack near the door was a stiff straw hat with a sedate brown band.

I've sometimes wondered whether the mayor, on leaving office, took his collection along, or whether he left it there with his predecessor's unicycle. Past a certain point, do the honors matter anymore? Too many of them are earned sitting behind banquets of roast chicken that might have been made of cardboard. The mayoral limousine gets stuck in traffic too. Still, perhaps they help.

Both money and recognition can be comforting things in our society because they say how much you matter. They are not always accurate, of course. Van Gogh had neither, at least during his lifetime, and even the salary of the United States President is modest compared with that of various corporate board chairmen. Perhaps power itself is a more accurate measure. An executive counts the number of employees under him, a violinist the number of listeners at her last recital. How many lives are you affecting? What is your impact on the world?

The other question is, how intense is your impact? A mechanic on a Detroit assembly line who installs door handles on five hundred automobiles a day theoretically affects the lives of some five hundred people, but none of them really notices so his work seems meaningless. His sister, a kindergarten teacher by contrast, influences only a few people, mainly the children in her classroom, but influences them so strongly that her work is automatically of some importance.

The strongest impact most people ever have on one another is probably through love. This includes love between parent and child and also that quieter version, friendship, as well as the flaming version, romantic love. "This being in love is great," wrote Fitzgerald again, in one of his notebooks. "You get a lot of compliments and begin to feel you're a great guy." It's true, it's true—and much more besides. Two people who are in love with each other don't wonder whether their lives have meaning.

Exerting personal impact is hard work, of course,

and responsibility for what happens to other people, though at first it may feel heady, can be highly stressful, especially in some situations. The federal government hired a research team from the University of Michigan to evaluate the effects of stress on people working in the space flight program—not astronauts themselves, but the ground staff of engineers, scientists and administrators. Of these three groups, it was the administrators who were found to suffer the worst. This was particularly true during manned space flights, as compared with unmanned ones. The administrators' serum cholesterol, blood sugar and blood pressure rose expecially high when they were responsible for human beings up there. But whatever their assignment, they had higher pulse rates and blood pressure and smoked more than either the engineers or the scientists—and they suffered almost three times as many heart attacks. Responsibility for people, concluded the report, always causes more stress than responsibility for things.

Studies of warfare in Korea and Vietnam confirm the point. Surprisingly, it was not the enlisted man or even the low-ranking non com whose internal bodily functions were most disturbed by combat, but people of higher rank, such as company grade officers, responsible for sending their men into a field of fire. Even medical corpsmen in helicopters, risking their lives to rescue crashed pilots, were able to rationalize their work. The officers back at the aid stations, in less danger, showed greater strain in the conventional physical indices of stress.

Nevertheless, people go on pursuing power, just as they pursue money and fame, and with good reason. These ingredients of so-called worldly success are not only reassuring, they are our best practical means for gaining the world's attention. They give us the chance to speak our piece, to say something with our lives.

So we struggle hard for them—sometimes so hard that we forget about the second problem.

The second problem is: What have you got to say? What are you going to do with the power? How are you going to spend the money? What's your point? If you don't know, you suffer from the malady known in the pulpits as "mere" worldly success. You've got the impact you wanted, but there's no you there to exert it.

The concept of identity—of the sense of self—is much bandied about in psychiatric journals, often quite abstrusely, but there is nothing necessarily mysterious about it. You are the way you are because of a whole list of specifics: what you want out of life; what you believe in; your emotional reactions; what you look like; your bodily responses in various situations; your talents; and so forth. Some of these specifics you are born with, like the shape of your hands; some, like your beliefs, are acquired through experience. Most are at least modified by experience.

From infancy onward, society modifies self—a good thing on the whole. A newborn baby is a squalling megalomaniac. It is society that turns infants, twenty-one years later, into more or less competent and rational adults. But sometimes the process goes too far. The need to get along, to be accepted, to succeed, becomes so important that bit by bit pieces of self are sacrificed until not very much is left. You learn to smile when you are really angry; you get your nose changed; you give up an eccentric hobby; you read the right books and say the right things about them. Pretty soon not much can be seen of you anymore but a bundle of correct reactions.

Self is not actually destroyed by this process. But it loses the chance to grow. It remains undeveloped, primordial. Driven underground, it can become an enemy. One of the ways it attacks you is stress, including physical stress disease.

If your temperament happens to fit the mores of your society, you're lucky: go ahead, enter the corporation, aim for the top job, have the two children and bring them up right, and all the rest. But what if it doesn't? Do you follow the same path anyway, fitting yourself in as best you can? This can sometimes be done, but past a certain point the costs exceed the profits. Skill and intelligence aside, some people aren't equipped for the big managerial jobs—responsibility erodes them. Some aren't equipped for parenthood—often for the same reason. Some aren't equipped for marriage. People have got to bend to the culture, obviously. But they must also make the culture bend to them, force it to make room for themselves as they really are. Living in society is a reciprocal matter, a constantly shifting relationship between the *you* and the *they*. When the balance is right you learn, you grow, you mean something.

Human personality has its bright side and its dark side, and people tend to concentrate on the first while doing their best to ignore the second. You express joy freely; anger you swallow. You welcome hope; you fight down fear. You cultivate your assets; your deficits you conceal as best you can. All this makes sense in a way, particularly in the world of work. The composer writes music and the athlete plays baseball, not the other way around. You do what you're good at—and what you're good at is of course intimately bound up with your sense of self.

It makes sense, but when it is carried too far life becomes constricted, and again, very stressful. Beauty queens have intellects too. A scholar has muscles. Our equipment is designed for use. If we don't use it, it can rebel and start using us.

This is especially true of the emotions. Like arms and legs, fear and anger are part of the basic human equipment: exercise develops them and makes them

useful. A person who is good at solving problems is a
person who knows how to be angry. He has learned to
use anger to change a situation.

It is when situations refuse to yield that people are
most inclined to bury their emotions—the very time,
often, when they most need to express them. Not all
problems can be solved, but almost all of them can be
relieved by the simple strategy of talking about them,
with feeling. It is not necessary to scream primally or
to break dishes in a Greek tavern, but it is vital to
phrase your frustrations, to get them out and hear
them, even if no one else listens.

I have a friend, a functioning member of the take
society, whose prescription for stress, if somewhat wag-
gish, has the virtue of being totally self-administered,
eliminating any need to attach wires to the head, or take
medications, or even see a therapist.

When he comes home from work after a bad day he
goes into his bedroom, closes the door, and takes out
one of those inexpensive portable tape recorders from
Japan. Then he opens the door to his closet. Pinned
to the inside, beside his exercise chart, is a list of
questions which, after setting the tape rolling, he re-
peats aloud, then answers into the microphone.

Among the questions:

1. Well, old victim, what did they do to you today,
   and who bit deepest?
2. Do you think Maureen (the wife) will want to make
   love tonight? Do you think you will want to?
3. Did the children look up when you came into the
   house? One child? Two? All three? If not, what do
   you suppose is eating them?
4. Feeling older or younger today?
5. What are you going to do tomorrow about what
   happened today?
6. How do you think death is going to come—describe
   your guess of how it will happen to you.

Having spoken answers to these and/or other questions on the list, he takes a quick shower, sits down and closes his eyes, meditates for twenty minutes, and goes downstairs into the kitchen and mixes himself just one martini, a 3½-ounce one.

There is more than rueful wit to my friend's exercise. He does speak out his problems, sometimes passionately, and he feels he leaves them behind to some degree when he goes downstairs to the refrigerator. He doesn't seem to have any ulcers, despite those martinis. Rarely does he save the tape to play back to himself at a later date. Instead, he takes the cassette out of the machine, places it under his underwear in a drawer, and erases it the next time he does the evening recitative. He refers to his machine as Dr. Sony, and has been recommending the routine to his wife too.

Talking is therapeutic at all ages, and need not always be angry or otherwise passionate. Sometimes older people can regain a sense of what they really are, of the story of their lives, by looking backward and talking to each other about the way things were when they were young. Elderly ladies, especially, are famous for long phone calls to old friends. On the phone they play back the roles of their youth to each other, reaching back in their stoutness to the slim girls they once were. It is a sound instinct, because early friends do fill out one another's lives in a unique way. In youth friends find friends by fitting into personality gaps in each other. One person's shyness is filled by the other's assertiveness; innocence by worldliness; imagination by practicality. People grow up and the underlying structure is obscured by the acquired skills and scars of adulthood, but they can remember the old roles, and regrasp them.

Theoretically, life should enlarge as you get older, as your competence and knowledge accumulate. Yet all too often it begins to narrow at what seems a very

premature point—in the thirties or forties, sometimes
even in the twenties. The vitality is still high, the brain
cells all functioning, but the possibilities close down
and the personality stops growing. Just a few years
ago you were a long-haired blonde who liked the Marx
Brothers, played a good game of gin rummy, and as-
pired to partnership in the law firm where you worked.
You may even have achieved that goal, yet today you
feel a little like a wind-up toy, obediently going
through motions. The *you* is fading out of your life.
Habit is fading in.

Perhaps what happens is that the first part of life is
mainly occupied by the quest for identity. According
to psychologists the individual personality sets very
early, and after the age of three no major changes are
likely: you are already you. Yet it remains to be discovered what this *you* is. What am I really like? is a
universally fascinating question, and in pursuit of the
answer almost any kind of change or challenge becomes welcome. Violin lessons; a hurricane; pneumonia; even war—anything new helps you find out
more about yourself.

Gradually the answers trickle in. Some are a pleasant surprise. Some are a little disappointing. Some are
painful. But finally a day comes when there don't seem
to be any major questions left to ask. You know what
you are, for better and for worse. And something very
important goes out of life.

Habit is essential to sane living. It gets you to work
on time. It helps you to keep hold of yourself in emergencies. It is also one way of defining and expressing
self: you are the kind of person who takes a shower
before breakfast, who reads the *Times* instead of the
News, watches the Late Show every night. Habits are
easy. Habits are reassuring. We all use them.

We use them, and go on using them, and then one
day wake up and discover that they have taken over

and are using us. We have become a set of responses, out of contact with the world, only half alive.

In these circumstances habit, designed to protect us from stress, becomes stressful itself. When a new situation comes along, you must see it as it really is and respond accordingly. Otherwise an opportunity is missed, or a problem goes unsolved. Habit seldom solves problems, and almost never seizes opportunities. It blinds itself to both. It is a substitute for spontaneous, felt action—a way of saying: You can't touch me, world.

But the world has got to touch us, just as we must touch it, if our lives are to say anything. And when we break through the habits, it does touch us and we become human again. A week in San Francisco will do it, away from the routine rounds of office and home. So will a reunion with a childhood friend. So will a confrontation with the eternal—in church, if you like, or perhaps on a mountain or a lonely stretch of beach. Sailing, skiing, ice skating, even a long walk, add the lyric quality to life. Even pet animals can help—cats, for instance. They aren't Americans. They aren't even people. But they have their own way of being successful—and a very clear sense of self.

Parents with young children especially need to sneak off by themselves at intervals and rediscover what their life together is about, besides meals, report cards and home carpentry.

If you know how to make the small changes, the big ones come a little easier. These are the changes that our lives depend on: the showdown with the wife or husband in an ebbing marriage, or with an employer in a job that has gone bad. Both marriages and jobs are sometimes saved by such showdowns. Sometimes they are broken. Sometimes they need to be broken. But individuals do not break, if they know how to change.

* * *

An important rule is, don't be meek. On the job the meek compete only by working harder, longer, faster, more slavishly. They take care not to evidence dislike of anyone; he or she may be their boss tomorrow. At home they don't raise their voices for fear of scarring the children's lives. They are meek in the subway, the grocery store, in traffic, with garage mechanics, appliance repairmen and those emperors, the civil servants. Above all the meek are meek in their marriages. They are careful never to place blame. Mentioning anything will only make it worse.

The meek shall inherit the earth? No, more likely ulcerative colitis.

If meekness is unconditional surrender, anger can be a kamikaze tactic. Seemingly the easiest way to control anger is to turn it off, to become a teetotaler, but that is only a short-term solution. Emotions don't go away. They build up slowly, and eventually a day comes when release is necessary. You blow up, yell or scream, perhaps weep, or hit someone. After that you shut it all off again for another long period. What is wrong with this method?

Two things. First, anger handled in this fashion changes from a useful, energetic property into a damaging one. A sudden eruption into rage, after months or years of suppression, can devastate the person who experiences it. Maybe in fury a husband struck his wife, or a wife walked out on her husband; or either quit a good job; or destroyed an important friendship. Looking about them at the wreckage, they say bleakly to themselves, "God, I can't afford to do that again." The next time around they may release the anger by getting sick, or depressed, or both.

More important, this method of handling anger—long periods of suppression interspersed by occasional outbursts—doesn't accomplish anything. It doesn't go to work on the situations that bring on the anger in the first place.

It is important to remember that anger itself is neither good nor bad for people. The real question is not even whether to express it or not; express it you must, one way or another. Aim to use it to improve things. When anger is regarded as a wild animal that must be caged, of course it becomes damaging. Only when you accept it as a natural response to difficult situations of many kinds can it then develop into a constructive tool. Anger, after all, is what rouses you to challenge a situation, and it is important to be able to act early on this anger, and to make those challenges. If you do so regularly the anger doesn't build up to unmanageable proportions. But even more important, it works *for* you. Often, with its help, you can change things. Sometimes you can't, of course, but even then the challenge is worth making. You have expended the anger, and perhaps you have learned something. Perhaps you have even changed a little yourself.

The business of life is to keep changing, a fact that all children know but which adults are apt to lose sight of, particularly as they grow older and their fears begin to outweigh their hopes. Is it that final change, death, that we really fear? And fearing death, do we come to fear living too? Erich Fromm* was writing about suicide, as well as success, when he said:

> A new question has arisen in modern man's mind, the question, namely, whether "Life is worth living" and correspondingly, the feeling that one's life "is a failure" or "is a success." The idea is based on the concept of life as an enterprise which should show a profit. The failure is like the bankruptcy of a business in which the losses are greater than the gains. This concept is nonsensical. We may be happy or unhappy, achieve some aims, and not achieve others; yet there is no sensible balance which would show whether life

*Erich Fromm, *The Sane Society*, Rinehart, 1955.

is worth living. It ends necessarily with death; many of our hopes are disappointed; it involves suffering and effort; from a standpoint of balance, it would seem to make more sense not to have been born at all, or to die in infancy. On the other hand, who can tell whether one happy moment of life, or the joy of breathing or walking on a bright morning and smelling the fresh air, is not worth all the suffering and effort which life implies? Life is a unique gift and challenge, not to be measured in terms of anything else, and no sensible answer can be given to the question whether it is "worth while" living, because the question does not make any sense.

EPILOGUE

A Second Chance

Becoming a parent means for most people another try at the world. Not everything works out the way we want in our own lives, but it's going to be different, we decide, for our sons and daughters: we'll see to that. So it is with hope, but also with a certain anxiety, that we watch them grow and slowly turn into adults themselves.

In the process, children gradually develop a way of being sick, as individual as their smile or their way of moving. What influences these patterns of illness, and what can we do about them, given our own patterns that we find so hard to alter?

Naturally, we try to feed them properly, see that they get enough exercise and rest, and administer the proper remedies when they fall ill. But from the beginning, underlying attitudes creep in and complicate the picture. It is when children get sick that these inner attitudes really come to the fore. First of all, even if the illness is only a cold the parent becomes somewhat disturbed. Colds can develop into bronchitis, or pneumonia, or rheumatic fever, and besides, the household routine is upset. Secondly, children themselves become more susceptible. Illness weakens their psychological defenses, and they are suddenly cut off from customary outlets: school, friends, the dime store, the library, the vacant lot down the street. They are shut in alone with themselves and a parent. Suddenly they feel much younger, almost like babies again. It is quite pleasant, but they know that the whole business of their lives is to grow older and more independent. And how a parent reacts to this situation may make matters worse. If children are babied in illness, that makes them uncomfortable, but if they are treated like malingerers that bothers them too. Illness creates a certain cycle of feelings: enjoyment of the easy, dependent way of life; guilt over the enjoyment; and expiation of the guilt through the pain and discomfort of symptoms. It is a cycle that holds together, that works. It works so well that in some people it becomes a lifelong pattern.

This doesn't mean a parent can't be sympathetic, for sick children are both lonely and vaguely upset. But when you visit with them, don't fall back on stories about how dear they were at age two. Talk about how they are going to spend the summer, or what they're accomplishing in school. And see that they have things to do—responsible tasks that will remind them of their basic capability and independence. They can organize their baseball cards, or cut up celery and carrots for the soup. If they're old enough, you can teach them to take their own temperature, or perhaps to measure out their medicine.

A word about medicine: don't use it unless you have a real reason. Aspirin, for example, reduces pain and fever, but it does so by suppressing the inflammatory reaction, and the inflammatory reaction is one way the body gets rid of disease-causing microbes. Sometimes, of course, the symptoms get out of hand—medicine makes sense for a fever of 103 degrees, or when coughing keeps a child awake at night. But in most illnesses the symptoms indicate that the body is at work fighting its disease, and the best strategy is not to interfere with its efforts.

Medicine is also habit-forming—any medicine, if you take enough of it, regardless of whether it happens to be physically addictive. A person whose childhood was highlighted by frequent dosings of one kind or another, held out in a spoon by a loving parent, is the kind of person who in adult life may go in for daily laxatives, nasal decongestants, vitamin pills, sedatives, psychic energizers, and the rest of the vast cornucopia worked up for him by today's drug industry. Drugs become what the psychoanalysts call Sources of Supply, and they help perpetuate that cycle of dependency, guilt and atonement through pain that can make illness so meaningful.

If drugs can keep the cycle going round, so can that more drastic medical remedy, surgery. Avoid it if you can, where your children are concerned. And if you can't, you must prepare them for it with particular care.

It helps to realize the special kinds of worries that an operation arouses in children. Naturally they worry about pain, and sometimes about death, just as adults do—in fact some young children, asked to define death, will say that it means going to the hospital. More than adults they worry about certain dreaded hospital procedures like shots and enemas.

They worry about being away from home and being taken care of by strangers, who may not have their true interests at heart. They also worry about being brave in such a setting—and with good reason. Cheerful patients make life easier for hospital personnel, who therefore encourage such an attitude, but whether it benefits patients themselves is debatable. A child who weeps from pain and loneliness after an essential operation should not be made to feel cowardly or babyish—he or she feels grief, and is better off acknowledging it.

The prospect of anesthesia disturbs many children, some of whom continue to worry about it even after they have recovered from successful surgery. They are left with a vague fear that something unknown was done to them while they were unconscious on the operating table, something they can neither see nor feel but which will be with them all their lives.

When you talk to your child about the operation he or she is going to have, it is important to be factual and clear about the procedures involved, as well as calm about the outcome. Tell them they will hurt afterwards, but will gradually feel better, and when this happens there will be other kids to play with and special things for children to do on their floor.

You should not only prepare the child, you had better prepare yourself, too—in particular for that moment when he is wheeled back from the recovery room to his bed. Even a twenty-minute tonsillectomy can do it, but the longer he was in surgery the worse he will look. His face will be white, his hair limp with dried sweat; through half-open lids his eyes will gaze sightlessly ahead without recognizing you. Don't burst into tears. In an hour he will begin to look alive again.

Feelings about sickness are not dictated solely, or even chiefly, by a child's experience with assorted stomach upsets, infections and operations: patterns of health are the result of far wider influences.

Who are the people who get the stress diseases?

First, they are afraid of their own feelings, particularly the feeling of anger, which they bury deep within, where it smolders unseen, eventually igniting the body's physical apparatus.

Secondly, they are in one way or another failures in life. Some are openly so—the "helpless-hopeless" type that George Engel wrote about, or the typical cancer patient of Dr. LeShan's study. Others, like the coronary personality, may be highly successful by twentieth-century business standards, but they are too constricted and too driven to be really alive. When people fail, they try to justify their failures, and many of them do so by getting sick. They also seek compensation—and many find it in being taken care of by their mates, by their local hospital, or by their insurance company. Convinced that they cannot get what they really want from life, they stop trying and aim instead for the next best thing: a salve for their bitter disappointment.

They also, very frequently, reach out for their children—the second-chance syndrome in its fullest and most sinister flower. Perhaps we have not really failed after all; if our children succeed then *we* will have succeeded, since we produced the children. In this fashion our hopes revive and we go to work, forcing opportunities on them, rousing in them the right ambitions and expectations, molding them, scolding them.

This can be very hard on children, particularly when you practice one thing and preach another. You advise them to be aggressive in life—when you yourself can't handle anger. You've got a little drinking problem—so you warn them off alcohol. You tell them how important a college degree is—you don't have one, and look how it's held you back. The message is confusing—and to children, disturbing. How can they go out and win the world when the two strongest people they know, their parents, can't win it?

It may bother you that your seventeen-year-old daughter dresses drably and has no interest in boys, but you can hardly scold her for that. So instead, when she is late coming home for dinner you chew her out as if she had committed a crime. Or perhaps your son, whom you have envisioned from birth as one day turning into an eminent cardiologist, gets mostly C's on his report card. Maybe his abilities and inclinations all point to a career as a garage mechanic. So what do you do when he gets into trouble? You tell him he can't take that job pumping gas at the Exxon station this summer.

This kind of thing happens all the time, the product of that second-chance syndrome so common to parenthood. But how can children live up to such expectations? And even if they can, should they? Will they "succeed" as a result? If the answers are cloudy, the solution isn't punishment; the solution may be to alter the expectations.

Punishing children for one thing when you are really angry about something else seldom gets results. It also does something to the children at the receiving end. Badness and inadequacy get mixed up in their minds, and both become an established part of their sense of self. The inadequacy they can't do much about, but the badness they can. They can feel guilty. And feeling guilty, they can aim for atonement. Atonement, they know from experience, comes through punishment; then reconciliation follows, and they are back where they started: the cycle is complete, with momentum remaining to begin again. For many people this becomes a lifelong pattern of unproductive behavior. In adulthood, away from parents, such people learn to punish themselves, often through illness.

Sometimes from the experience of illness we learn to be sick. And from the experience of failure, we learn to fail. And from the experience of being unable to control ourselves, we learn that we are beyond control. This is the kind of learning children can do without.

Children's lives, including their problems, belong to them, not to the parent, and a parent's task is to help them learn to manage these problems. They will need anxiety, to help them recognize the problems. They will need anger, to help them find solutions. They will need grief, to help dispel their failures. And they will need to develop and train these emotions, just as they develop and train their bodies and their intellects. If all goes well, they will turn out to be not star athletes, perhaps, or world leaders, or great physicians, but something better: adults at home with the world and with their families, physically healthy, able to take failure, able to take success—alive, and glad to be alive.

APPENDIX

A Predictive Study of Coronary Heart Disease

THE WESTERN COLLABORATIVE GROUP STUDY

Ray H. Rosenman, M.D., Meyer Friedman, M.D.,
San Francisco, Calif.,
Reuben Straus, M.D., Moses Wurm, M.D.,
Robert Kositchek, M.D., Burbank, Calif.,
Wilfrid Hahn, Ph.D., and
*Nicholas T. Werthessen, Ph.D., San Antonio, Tex.**

PROCEDURES FOR ASSESSMENT OF BEHAVIOR PATTERN

A. Personal Interview—It is our belief that behavior pattern A arises in a subject when he is more or less *continuously* involved in a conflict or struggle in which he is determined to persevere. Sometimes the "adversary" in this conflict which involves the subject with behavior pattern A is one or more individuals (e.g., a competitive rival, an oppressive superior, an antagonistic member of the family, etc.), but by far the most frequent "adversary" is the seeming paucity of time itself. Perhaps intrinsically oriented to the desire for

* Drs. Rosenman and Friedman are from the Harold Brunn Institute of Mount Zion Hospital and Medical Center; Drs. Straus, Wurm, and Kositchek from the research laboratories of St. Joseph Hospital; and Drs. Hahn and Werthessen from the Southwest Foundation for Research and Education.
  Reprinted by permission of the authors.

an ever-increasing number of achievements, the typical subject with pattern A may have the ability to bring this about if he had sufficient time. But so unbridled are his desires that invariably he finds himself partially frustrated or in conflict with time itself. Moreover, this last conflict is one in which he accepts neither defeat nor compromise. Accordingly, detection of behavior pattern A consists in determining whether a subject is in *active and continuous* conflict either with other subjects or with time. Such detection could be made by observation of various motor, emotional, and intellectual attributes which become part and parcel of behavior pattern A.

After preliminary studies in which various standard and other written psychological questionnaires were employed, it was found by us that a personal interview (recorded on magnetic tape for deliberate study) was pre-eminently the tool of choice for the detection of the type A behavior pattern. It was found to have at least three advantages over any written questionnaire. It allowed the interviewer, first, to observe the all-important motor activities of the subject and, second, to observe and assess the intensity and quality of emotional change and overtones accompanying the intellectual response of the interviewee to each propounded question. Thus, such indications of pattern A as speech hurrying, explosive accentuations in the ordinary rhythm of speech, and nascent vibrancy and aggressive timbre of a voice, can all be detected by the interviewer and recorded upon the magnetic tape. Third, the personal interview allowed the questioner facility, flexibility, and variability in his approach to a subject when such was needed to uncover or classify more accurately certain personality attributes of a given subject. Certainly, it cannot be stressed too greatly that *the correct classification of a subject depended far more upon the motor and emotional qualities accompanying his response to specific questions than the ac-*

tual content of his answers. To minimize or to misunderstand this last differential is to fail in the correct behavioral assessment of a subject.

Accordingly, during the personal interview four general entities were investigated: (1) presence of characteristic motor signs (2) degree of drive and ambition (3) degree of past and present competitive, aggressive, and hostile feelings and (4) degree of intensity of sense of time urgency.

Detection of Presence of Characteristic Motor Signs—Obviously a man constantly oppressed by the scarcity of time seemingly available to him eventually hastens all or most of his physical actions such as walking, talking, and eating and when slowed by ambient forces is most likely to express irritation by body restlessness. So commonplace, so commonsensical are these reactions that they have been overlooked and minimized heretofore.

Again, a man in conflict with other individuals or even with himself is apt to exhibit expressive motor signs (e.g., a scowl or grimace or a clenched hand) when this conflict is even referred to retrospectively.

Therefore, before and during the personal interview, the following observations upon each subject were made and recorded by the interviewer: (1) degree of mental and emotional alertness (minimal, average, extreme) (2) speed of local motion (minimal, average, extreme) (3) body restlessness (none, average, extreme) (4) facial grimaces (scowls, teeth-clenching, and tic in which teeth are clenched and masseter muscles are tensed) (5) hand movements (fist-clenching, gestures made with extraordinary vigor, e.g., desk-pounding).

Degree of Drive and Ambition—The following questions were asked each subject by the interviewer and their responses were assessed just as much or even more by the manner in which they answered the questions as by the actual content of their replies.

(1) Were you on any athletic or other teams or activities in high school or college? (If affirmative) What teams were you captain of? (If negative, ascertain whether subject strove to lead the teams and/or activities in which he engaged.)

(2) Since you began making your living did you or do you now go to night school or other school to *improve* your chances of advancement?

(3) Are you *satisfied* with your present job? (If affirmative) When younger did you *consciously* strive for advancement? (If negative) Do you *still strive* to advance?

(4) Do you have more than one job? Do you belong to any community or civic activities? Are you an officer of any of these organizations?

Typically, the man with pattern A will be found to have (1) played on high school athletic teams (2) gone to night, or other further, school (3) be dissatisfied with remaining in his present position and (4) participate in various organizations.

Degree of Past and Present Competitive, Aggressive, and Hostile Feelings—The following questions were asked to determine the degree of intensity of these emotional facets.

(5) Do you think of yourself as hard-driving and aggressive, or as relaxed and easygoing? What does your wife think?

(6) Do you strive for the *admiration and respect* of your friends and working associates or for their affection?

(7) When you play games with your children (or, if there are none, with children of friends or relatives)

do you *purposely usually* let them win? (If negative answer) Did you *ever* let them win? Why?

(8) When you play athletic or card games with friends do you give *it all your worth,* in there *fighting all the way?* Do you play mainly *to win* or for the fun of it?

(9) Is there much *competition* in your work? Do you *enjoy* it? Do you *prefer* it?

(10) Are you a *fast* car driver? Up to the speed limit or just *beyond* it? Does it *irritate* you to be held up by a car in front of you? Do you try to *move* him out of the way? What do you say? Does your wife usually try to slow you down?

(11) Do you frequently get upset? Get angry? Do you usually show it or do you try to keep it inside of you?

The subject with behavior pattern A in answering these questions sometimes may not think of himself as hard driving and aggressive, but invariably he will admit that his wife believes he is (5). He typically prefers respect and admiration to affection (6). He rarely allows his children to win at any game (7). He always plays to win (8) and he finds and enjoys competition (9). He becomes inordinately irritated at any driver obstructing his passage (10). Although he frequently angers, he goes out of his way to conceal such feelings (11). Here again the emotional overtones accompanying his responses are to be valued above his actual responses in words.

Degree of Intensity of Sense of Time Urgency—Since we believe that it is this particular emotional distress that more than any other irritates, sustains, and intensifies pattern A, the major portion of the interview is devoted to the elicitation of the presence of factors that either may lead to the sense of time urgency or serve as indicators of its already established presence. Ten questions are asked for the importance of the possible content of the responses and two additional questions are asked solely to observe the presence or absence of speech hurrying in the response.

Content Questions

(12) Are there many *deadlines* in your work? Do you enjoy them? Are they *exciting?* Do you find that you get more done working against deadlines?

(13) When you have an appointment to meet your wife or a friend somewhere, will you be there *on time*? Do you *like* to work up to the last moment to *get more done* before leaving to keep an appointment? Does it *bother you* if you are kept waiting? If so, what do you do about it?

(14) How much time do you spend on hobbies? Is this only when you have nothing *more important* to do?

(15) Do you *like* to help your wife with dishes and housekeeping or do you resent this as a waste of time? Or do you prefer to *accomplish* your own projects around the house?

(16) Do you get *impatient* when you see something being done at home or at work *slower* than you think it should be done?

(17) Do you often try to get *something else done,* like calculating or reading *trade* material when eating alone? Or while in the bathroom? Or while shaving?

(18) Do you *like* to walk *fast*? After dinner at home do you like to *dawdle* around the table or do you *prefer* to eat *quickly* and get on to more important projects?

(19) Do you get *irritated* if you *have to wait* for a table in a restaurant? Do you wait? How about *waiting* in a bank line? Do you *plan* your eating out or going to a bank so that you won't have to wait?

(20) When someone is talking to you do you often find yourself thinking about other things? If he *takes too long* to get to the *point* do you feel like *hurrying*

him along to get to the point *faster*? Do you *put* words in *his* mouth?

(21) Do you often have the feeling that time is *passing too quickly* each day to get everything done that you want to? That time is passing you by? Does this sense of *time urgency* make you look at your watch often? Make you feel that you have to do *everything in a hurry*?

The subject with pattern A in answering these questions believes that he does have deadlines, but enjoys them (12). He is invariably punctual and it annoys him greatly if others keep him waiting (13). He rarely finds time to indulge in hobbies or if he does so they frequently are, or he makes them, as competitive and tension-rich as his vocation (14). He dislikes helping at home in routine jobs because he feels his time can be spent more profitably (15). He frequently prefers to do a job himself because he grows impatient watching the slower action of others (16). He shamefacedly admits that he is very apt to attempt to carry on work while eating, in the toilet, etc. (17). He walks fast and he rarely remains long at the dinner table (18). He invariably dislikes waiting for anything (19). He makes it a habit to attempt to carry on a second line of thought whenever he feels he can manage to get away with it, and he is extremely liable to arrive "at the end of a subject" long before the speaker discussing the subject will come to it (20). He feels almost constantly that time is passing too rapidly, that he must hurry, and he admits of frequent observations of his watch.

Admittedly, many subjects with pattern B might answer various questions with the same affirmative replies given by the subject with pattern A, but it is the manner in which the latter subject answers them which reveals the underlying sense of time urgency. For example, any individual might state that he likes to be punctual but the subject with pattern A will emphatically make such statements as "I am *never* late" or "I've *always* taken pride in being on time," and he will intensify his voice when pronouncing the italicized adverbs. Again even the subject with pattern B might dislike waiting in a restaurant or in a bank line but he does not "explode" verbally as do pattern A subjects with such statements as "I *hate* it," "I just *wouldn't* wait," "It is an *unnecessary imposition* on the customer," etc. Thus, perhaps in no category of questions is the audition of the type and quality of response so important as in this one in which the sense of time urgency is being assessed.

Questions to Elicit Speech Hurrying

Since as mentioned above, the subject with pattern A, having an extreme sense of time urgency, almost always attempts and usually succeeds in reaching the point of a question or a statement prior to the speaker propounding them, he is extremely likely to answer before the propounder finishes the question. This propensity (which is such a good indicator for the presence of time urgency) is searched for in the personal interview by proposing the following two questions.

(22) Most persons prefer to awaken and get up and get going before 9:00 A.M. Uh-what-time-uh-do you-uh, uh-uh uh-like to-uh-get up?

(23) Have you ever taken snapshots? Well, uh-when you did take them, uh-the films-uh, the development-uh-did you yourself-uh-uh-develop-uh-uh-them?

It will be observed that in question 22 the first sentence already alerts the subject to the fact that he is also going to be asked at what time he arises. The subject with pattern A, alert and impelled by a sense of time urgency, already has his answer and when the questioner seems to be stumbling in asking him, his impatience forces him to give the answer before the question is terminated. Similarly, in question 23, just as soon as the questioner stumblingly emits the word "development," the interviewee knows what the total specific question will be. The subject with pattern A at this juncture, however, will interrupt and say, "No, I didn't develop them," or "Did I develop them myself, no, I did not." Conversely, the subject with pattern B will wait until the interviewer has finished asking the question before expressing his reply.

The classification of the subject upon the basis of the personal interview thus depended upon his observed motor behavior and the emotional and intellectual tenor of his responses to the total series of questions.

Although it was relatively easy to classify the interviewed subjects as either exhibiting behavior pattern A or B, it was far more difficult to assess the degree of development of either pattern. Nevertheless, such subclassification was attempted.

A subject was assessed as exhibiting behavior pattern A-1 if he displayed the various above-described motor activities (e.g., hand-clenching, facial grimaces, body restlessness) and if his responses to the questions indicated that there was an extreme degree of emotional frustration concerned with or arising out of his excessive drives, ambitions, aggressions, hostilities, and source of time urgency. A subject was assessed as exhibiting pattern A-2 if he exhibited many but not all of these behavioral traits. A subject was assessed as exhibiting behavior pattern B-4, first, if he exhibited none of the characteristic motor signs associated with pattern A, secondly if he appeared to have no sense of time urgency as well as a minimum of drive and ambition which possibly might have given rise to a sense of time and urgency, and thirdly, if he was not found to harbor any obvious hostility against friend, associate, or relative. An individual was assessed as behavior pattern B-3 if, while not exhibiting motor activity or an obvious sense of time urgency, he nevertheless exhibited some drive and ambition.

B. Psychophysiological Test—The second procedure employed to aid in the detection and assessment of the behavior pattern was subjection of each subject to a specially designed psychophysiological test. A polygraph similar to the type used in "lie detection tests" was employed to record graphically various physiological functions and motor actions of each subject while he was required to listen to a sixteen-minute tape recording of two monologues. One of these monologues was delivered by a man speaking evenly, forcefully, and at the usual conversational rate about a subject of general interest. However, this monologue was interrupted on eleven occasions by a "challenge" monologue delivered in a slow, irritatingly hesitant, stumbling, and repetitive manner by a young woman and was concerned with a trivial, totally inane subject. This "challenge" monologue almost invariably allowed the listener to foretell the end of each sentence before it actually was spoken. Needless to say, such a monologue proves to be especially irritating and reaction-evoking in most individuals suffering from a sense of time urgency.

The physiological functions graphically recorded were the rate and character of respirations measured both at the level of the second and third intercostal spaces and at the seventh and eighth intercostal level. The motor reactions which were graphically recorded were any movement of the hands, legs, or body and any clenching of the fist.

As described previously (16), the average younger patient with coronary artery disease, while listening to a longer version of the same tape recording, sharply differentiated himself from the normal subject exhibiting behavior pattern B. Thus he either moved restlessly or breathed abnormally at least once every forty seconds of listening time. Also, his upper chest breathing became more prominent than that of his lower chest and he was observed to inspire air at a far more rapid rate than the control subject. Finally, more often than not, he would indulge in fist-clenching during the audition.

The assessment of the polygram was done by one of us (M. F.) who had no other knowledge of the subject tested. In the present study a subject was considered to possess pattern A (subclassification A-1) if he displayed all of the above described phenomena that had been noted in the majority of the previously studied patients with behavior pattern A. If, however, he only exhibited several of these phenomena (but always including the frequent occurrence of respiratory or motor reactions), he was classified as A-2.

On the other hand, if a subject exhibited a motor or respiratory activity less frequently than once every 125 seconds or longer during the audition, if his diaphragmatic respiratory excursion always exceeded that of his upper chest, if his inspiration of air was slow, and if he did not indulge at all in fist-clenching, he was considered to exhibit pattern B (sub-classification B-4). If, however, a subject did exhibit body activity and respiratory abnormalities more frequently than once every 125 seconds but less than once every 90 seconds, or more prominent upper than lower chest breathing, or a rapid inspiratory rate, he was classified usually as pattern B-3. It should be noted that hand-clenching was never observed in subjects unless they also displayed very frequent body movements and respiratory abnormalities.

Admittedly, absolute quantitative precision in assessment by this means was not feasible. But it was believed that the information obtained by this procedure might prove to be of some value in deciding the final overall assessment and predictive classification of each subject.

FURTHER READING

Any single book on the subject of stress is by necessity only a beginning. In these notes we recommend, out of our own research experience, a number of sources the reader can pursue in order to expand his understanding. It is a compact list, narrowed—with just a few exceptions—to works that are easily obtainable. Very few medical papers are listed. They are too hard to come by and often too technical for the lay reader, and we therefore mention only those that we consider essential in their message, unduplicated in more general discussions in books.

On the subject of stress in general:

Stress and Disease by Harold G. Wolff; edited by Stewart Wolf (Springfield, Illinois: Charles C. Thomas, 1953). A particularly sound exposition. Some pages are a bit technical, but more than worth your careful attention.

Man's Presumptuous Brain by A.T.W. Simeons (New York: E. P. Dutton, 1961). Designed for a general readership, this is a lucid and often entertaining account of the role of the diencephalon in physical disease by a British physician who is not afraid to follow his hunches. Particularly good on afflictions in the digestive tract.

The Physiology and Pathology of Exposure to Stress by Hans Selye (Montreal: Acta, 1950). Long, highly technical, and available only in medical libraries, but a truly definitive work. For readers with an already thorough knowledge of human physiology.

The Stress of Life by Hans Selye (New York: Mc-Graw, 1956). A popularized exposition of Selye's work. Still quite technical, but essential reading for anyone seriously interested in the subject.

The preceding books emphasize the physical mechanisms in stress disease. Its psychological aspects—the role played by personality and emotion—occupy center stage in the following:

Stress by Lennart Levi (New York: Liveright, 1967).

Psychological Development in Health and Disease by George L. Engle (Philadelphia: W. B. Saunders, 1962). How emotional patterns turn up in physical behavior and can help lead to illness.

Psychomatic Research: A Collection of Papers by J. J. Groen et al (New York: Macmillan, 1964). The report of a group of Dutch doctors concerning their work with patients at a hospital in Amsterdam. A sober, detailed study with particularly good material on asthma.

Psychosomatic Diagnosis by Flanders Dunbar (New York: Harper, 1943). A psychiatrist's lengthy but fascinating investigation of 1,600 random patients at Columbia Presbyterian Hospital some fifty years ago. Particularly strong on cardiovascular diseases and the accident-prone.

Mind and Body: Psychosomatic Medicine by Flanders Dunbar (New York: Random, 1947). A short easy-to-read, "popular" explanation of the psychosomatic point of view, but less convincing than the author's other work.

Psychosomatic Medicine by Edward Weiss and O. Spurgeon English (Philadelphia: W. B. Saunders, 1943). A sound and thorough work with a textbook tone.

Psychosomatic Medicine: Its Principles and Applications by Franz Alexander (New York: W. W. Norton, 1950). Clear and well written, by a noted psychoanalyst, with interesting material on respiratory disease, hyperthyroidism, rheumatoid arthritis, and afflictions of the lower digestive tract.

Psychological Aspects of Physical Symptoms by Samuel Silverman (New York: Appleton-Century-Crofts, 1968). Also by a psychoanalyst. Many case histories.

Society, Stress and Disease, Volume 1: The Psychosocial Environment and Psychosomatic Diseases, edited by Lennart Levi (New York: Oxford University Press, 1971). Research in stress, a relatively new field of investigation, is still only loosely coordinated. To rectify this situation a series of international conferences was instituted, the first of which was held in Stockholm, Sweden, in 1970 under the sponsorship of the World Health Organization and the University of Uppsala. The proceedings and papers are reported completely here. The volume runs to 500 packed pages and is an impressive view of the research then being done in the field.

The following works deal with specific areas of stress.

Cardiovascular:

Type A: Behavior and Your Heart by Meyer Friedman and Ray H. Rosenman (New York: Knopf, 1974). For lay readers, a description of the relation between personality and heart attack.

The Pathogenesis of Coronary Artery Disease by Meyer Friedman (The Blakiston Division of McGraw Hill, 1969). A somewhat more technical discussion of Dr. Friedman's specialty.

Digestive:

The Stomach by Stewart Wolf (New York: Oxford University Press, 1965). Not easy to find (it deserves to be reissued) but well worth a search. A moderately technical book on gastric function which the layman can not only understand but relish. Includes the adventures of Tom.

"Studies of Ulcerative Colitis—III: The Nature of the Psychologic Processes" by George L. Engel (printed in the *American Journal of Medicine* in August, 1955). A study of the life patterns common to ulcerative colitis patients.

Immunology:

Body and Antibody: A Report on the New Immunology by David Wilson (New York: Knopf, 1971). A clear and thorough study for laymen of the complex immunological system in human beings.

Natural History of Infectious Disease, 4th ed., by Sir McFarlane Burnet (New York: Cambridge University Press, 1972). Written by one of the all-time giants in immunology research, with great enthusiasm for his subject.

An excellent book on the general subject of cancer is *Cancer: The Wayward Cell. Its Origins, Nature and Treatment* by Victor Richards (Berkeley: University of California Press, 1972). But to grasp the role of stress in cancer, you really need to read the paper written by Lawrence LeShan which we quoted at length on pages 79 to 81. It is called "An Emotional Life-History Pattern Associated with Neoplastic Disease," and it was printed in the 1966 *Annals of the N.Y. Academy of Sciences*. It is a persuasive, first-rate job.

Headaches: Their Nature and Treatment by Stewart Wolf and Harold G. Wolff (Boston: Little, 1953). Describes the physiological and emotional processes in all varieties of headache.

Arthritis and You by James W. Brooke (New York: Harper, 1960). Not stress-oriented, but a thoughtful and thorough analysis of the many manifestations of this complex disease.

* * *

The following books do not deal directly with stress as such, but provide helpful background material on the general operations of mind and body. First, the mind:

Childhood and Society by Erik Erikson (New York: Norton, 1950). From infancy through old age, the eight psychosocial stages of human development. By a psychoanalyst with a penetrating grasp of what it means to be human.

The Meaning of Anxiety by Rollo May (New York: Ronald Press, 1950). A prevailing mood of our time, its causes and effects.

The Psychology of Melancholy by Mortimer Ostrow (New York: Harper & Row, 1970). A perceptive study of depression.

Human Aggression by Anthony Storr (New York: Atheneum, 1968). What it does for you, and to you.

Our Inner Conflicts by Karen Horney (New York: Norton, 1945). An eminent psychiatrist's view of the nature of neurosis.

In the area of human physiology one of the best single sources is still *The Wisdom of the Body* by Walter B. Cannon (New York: Norton). First published in 1932, this is a classic analysis of the many complex forces within the body and how they maintain equilibrium with one another.

For the lay reader, almost as highly recommended are the many works of science writer Isaac Asimov. His books are accurate, lucid, enthusiastic, and a pleasure to read. Among the most pertinent: *The Human Body: Its Structure and Operation* (Boston: Houghton Mifflin, 1963); *The Human Brain: Its Capacities and Functions* (New York: Houghton Mifflin, 1964); and *The Chemicals of Life: Enzymes, Vitamins, Hormones* (New York: Abelard-Schuman, 1954).

A good book on the nervous system is *The Communication System of the Body* by David F. Horrobin (New York: Basic Books, 1964).

On the endocrine system, try *Teach Yourself Hor-*

mones in Man and Animals by E. Otto Höhn (London: English Universities Press, 1966).

Another interesting book is *The Physiology of Hostility* by Kenneth E. Boyer (Chicago: Markham Publishing Company, 1971).

Also recommended: *Neurophysiology and Emotion*, edited by David C. Glass (New York: Rockefeller University Press and Russell Sage Foundation, 1967). An interesting, if often quite technical, collection of papers on the relation between emotions and the nervous and endocrine systems. Particularly outstanding is Stanley Schachter's study of overeating.

Understanding stress is one matter; doing something about it is another. But books are helpful here too.

Before you go on a diet, for instance, read *The Importance of Overweight* by Hilde Bruch (New York: Norton, 1957).

Before you embark on an exercise regimen try *Aerobics* by Kenneth Cooper (New York: M. Evans, distribued in association with Lippincott, 1968) or *The New Aerobics* by Kenneth Cooper (New York: M. Evans, distributed in association with Lippincott, 1970).

Available from the Federal government are several good exercise guides, the basic one being a publication of The President's Council on Physical Fitness and Sports entitled "Adult Physical Fitness." Others include: "Aerobic Dancing, Rhythmic Sport: Orginated and Choreographed by Jacki Sorensen," "Interval Training," "Jogging Guidelines," and "Physical Conditioning through Water Exercises," by C. Carson Conrad. The address of The President's Council on Physical Fitness and Sports is Washington, D.C. 20201.

If you're looking for a psychotherapist first spend some time with *The Comprehensive Textbook of Psy-*

chiatry, edited by Alfred M. Freedman and Harold I. Kaplan (Baltimore: Williams and Wilkins, 1967). It doesn't list practitioners but its 1,666 pages give a clear picture of the different schools of psychotherapy practiced today and can help you decide which one might serve you the best.

Another good background source: *The Mind of Man* by Walter Bromberg (New York: Lippincott, 1954). An excellent history of psychotherapy and psychoanalysis.

People interested in groups should read *Carl Rogers on Encounter Groups* by Carl Rogers (New York: Harper & Row, 1970), a work of wisdom and candor.

Those interested in consciousness expansion and similar techniques might well consult two books by Robert Ornstein, both of them able presentations of a wide span of adaptive psychological techniques ranging from meditation to negative ions in the air. The first, *The Psychology of Consciousness* (San Francisco: W. H. Freeman; New York: Viking, 1973) is Ornstein's own word on the subject; the second, *The Nature of Human Consciousness* (San Francisco: W. H. Freeman; New York: Viking, 1973) is an anthology of essays by many authorities. On a similar subject, and equally interesting, is *The Natural Mind* by Andrew Weill (Boston: Houghton Mifflin, 1972) which explains what expanded consciousness does for people, and why they take drugs for its sake, or give up drugs for meditation in order to achieve a finer "high."

Additional Reading, a note to the 1993 revised edition—The following books were published after *Stress* first came out in 1974. They have been culled from a long list of recent works in the field.

Head First, the Biology of Hope by Norman Cousins (New York: E.P. Dutton, 1989). Late in life this well-known writer and editor embarked on a second career by joining the UCLA Medical School, where he was able to pursue professionally a subject that had long fascinated him—the mind-body relationship and its effect on health. An articulate and persuasive survey of recent research.

Mind as Healer, Mind as Slayer by Kenneth R. Pelletier (New York: Delacorte Press, 1976). First published sixteen years ago, this careful, intelligent book by a California psychologist has become a classic in the field. Emphasis is on preventive techniques.

The Healing Brain: Breakthrough Discoveries About How the Brain Keeps Us Healthy by Robert Ornstein and David Sobel (New York: Simon and Schuster, 1987). Though at times awkwardly written, this book covers a great deal of extremely interesting research on the central nervous system and conveys the complexity of its subject without confusing a lay reader.

The Healer Within: The New Medicine of Mind and Body by Steven Locke, M.D., and Douglas Colligan (New York: E.P. Dutton, 1986). An excellent summation of recent work in the field of mind-brain-immune system relations.

The Trusting Heart by Redford Williams, M.D. (New York: Times Books, 1989). A good explanation of recent modification in the coronary-prone Type A personality profile, by a researcher in the field.

Dr. Dean Ornish's Program for Reversing Heart Disease by Dean Ornish, M.D. (New York: Random House, 1990). A serious, honest, highly persuasive explication of the author's system for halting, and in some cases reversing, coronary artery blockage. A long book, packed with specific instructions, including 146 pages of low-fat vegetarian recipes.

Full Catastrophe Living by Jon Kabat-Zinn, Ph.D. (New York: Delacorte Press, 1990). The author describes in detail the program of meditation, relaxation, and self-awareness which he originated and still runs at the University of Massachusetts Medical Center.

Patients who have benefited suffer from cardiovascular disease, cancer, chronic pain, pulmonary disease, and other stress-related conditions.

The Inner Game of Tennis by W. Timothy Gallway (New York: Random House, 1974). How to employ certain mental techniques to enhance concentration, dispel self-doubt, and become relaxed—all while attempting to hit a tennis ball. The advice may concern tennis, but it translates readily to most fields of human endeavor. Written with disarming simplicity.

INDEX

Accidents, Accident-proneness, 5, 90–96
  anger vs. aggression and, 94–96
ACTH (AdrenoCorticoTrophic Hormone), 110–111, 113, 114
Acupuncture, 193
Adrenal gland, 108, 112–114
Aerobics, 135, 136–138
Aerospace Medicine, 138
Aggression
  vs. dependency, 102–105
  hostile, 131
  pent-up drives, 132
  stress and, 114
Alcohol, Alcoholism, 39n, 173, 186–187
Alcoholics Anonymous, 182
Alexander, Franz, 72–73, 89, 99
  Psychosomatic Medicine, 55n
Allergy, stress and, 70–73
Aluminum Company of America, 152–153
American Medical Association, 177
Amsterdam, Holland, 71, 120
Anger, 121, 209–210

stress and, 214–215
Angina, 34, 42–43
  angina-prone person, 25
Angry nonparticipant type, 104
Antibiotics, 64
Antibodies, 64, 67–68, 69, 74–75
Antidepressants, 171, 172
Antigens, 67, 68, 70, 74, 78
Anxiety, 104–105
Arica, 187
Arrhythmia, 23, 34, 42–43, 178, 189
Arthritis, 5, 15, 73–75, 86–89, 120, 121
  immunology and, 63
  osteoarthritis, 87
  rheumatoid arthritis
    immune system and, 73–75
    stress, and, 87–89
Aslan, Dr. Ana, 198
Asthma, 5, 71–73, 120, 163
  hypnosis and, 193–194
Atlas, Charles, 133
Aura, 44
Authority, hypertensives and, 40
Auto-immunity, 74–75
Automobiles, accident involving, 95–96

Autonomic nervous system, 121, 188, 190, 192

Backache, 5, 84–86, 89, 103
Baltimore, Md., 189
Barbiturates, 170, 172
Barrett, Elizabeth, 199
Beatles, the, 183
Ben Gurion, David, 204
Benchley, Robert, 143
Benson, Dr. Herbert, 184–185
Berger, Hans, 190
Bernard, Claude, 3, 19
Bicycling, 137
Bio-feedback Research Society, 192
Biological feedback, 128, 188–193
Blood pressure
stress and, 37–39
see also Hypertension
Boston, Mass., 180, 187
Bowel disorders, 55–59
see also Colitis; Constipation; Diarrhea
Brain
biological feedback and, 190–193
organ of mind, 101
Breuer, Dr. Joseph, 159–160
Bromberg, Dr. Walter
The Mind of Man, 128
Brookline, Mass., 166
Brown, Dr. P. W., 57
Browning, Robert, 199
Bucharest, Rumania, 198
Budzynski, Dr. Thomas, 190

Cancer, 6, 220
immunology and, 63, 75–82
state of mind and, 79–82
stomach cancer, 54–55
stress and, 78–82

Cardiovascular system, 23–45
stress exercises, 134–136
see also cardiovascular diseases, e.g., Angina
Cells
cellular transplant theory, 198
differentiated vs. dedifferentiated, 78
Center for Studies of the Person, 181
Cerebral cortex, 107–108, 109
Change, 215–216
stress and, 12–13
Charcot, Dr. Jean, 159
Chicken pox, 70
Cholesterol studies, 23–24, 25–27, 30–32, 114, 156, 163
Christenson, William N., 73
Christian Science, 194
Churchill, Winston, 6
Clonal theory, 66–67
Cluff, Dr. Leighton, 174
Cobb, Sidney, et al.
"Why Do Wives with Rheumatoid Arthritis Have Husbands with Peptic Ulcers?" 52
Cocaine, 158, 171
Cold, common, 68–69
Colitis, 5, 162
ulcerative, 59–61, 75
Combat, mortal, 7
Constipation, 55, 56, 57
Cooper, Dr. Kenneth H., 135, 136–138, 141
Cornell, Dr. Albert, 177
Coronary disease, 119
coronary thrombosis, 6
coronary type, 34–37, 220
predictive study of, 224–235

Davis, Arthur Vining, 152–153

Death, 8, 215–216
  stress and, 123–124

Deferred obedience, 126

Dependency
  vs. aggression, 102–105
  breaking away from, 125–126
  vs. hostility, 160–161

Depression, 105

Di Cara, Leo V., 188

Diabetes, 15, 34, 119
  exercise and, 138

Diarrhea, 54, 55, 56, 57

Diet, Dieting, 143–157
  diet doctors, 153
  diet pills, 171, 172
  dieting clubs, 153
  Eastern meditation
    movements and, 185–186
  food fads, 147–149
  "health" foods, 156–157
  high protein diet, 149,
    150–151
  medical supervision of
    weight-reduction diet,
    149–156
  overeating, 143–145
  permissible deviations in
    dieting, 151–152

Digestive system, 46–48
  emotional stress and, 48–51

Diphenylhydantoin (DPH;
  Delantin), 175, 176

Diphtheria, 3

Disease
  chronic, 163–164
  disease-proneness, 220–221
  emotions and, 70–71, 119–126, 217–218
  infectious, 63–64
  "placebo effect" in cures
    of, 197

stress and, 4–7
  see also names of diseases

DPH, *see* Diphenylhydantoin

Dreyfus, Jack, 175–176

Drinking Man's Diet, 147

Drugs, 128, 169–179, 186–187
  antidepressants, 171
  controlled narcotics, 171
  diet pills, 171
  illegal drugs, 171–172
  nonbarbiturate sedatives,
    170
  pep pills, 171
  psychotropic, 169–174
  tranquilizers, 170–171
  see also Placebos; *names
    and classifications of
    drugs, e.g.* Barbiturates;
  Cocaine

Dunbar, Dr. Flanders, 90,
  94, 95, 121, 122
  heart disease studies, 34–37
  hypertension studies, 39,
    40, 41–42
  Psychosomatic Diagnosis,
    35n

Ectomorphs, 146

Eddy, Mary Baker, 159

Ego, 102

Emotions, 209–211
  illness and, 34, 119–126,
    163–169, 217–218
  vs. logic, 99–101

Emphysema, 5, 118

Encephalitis, 65

Encounter groups, 179–182

Endomorphs, 146

Engel, Bernard, 189

Engel, Dr. George, 104, 220

English, Dr. O. Spurgeon
  Psychosomatic Medicine
    (with Weiss), 52, 57–59

Epilepsy, 176

Erikson, Erik, 161
  Childhood and Society, 123n
Esalen movement, 181
Eskimo diet, 147–148
Exercise, 128
  hazards of, 138
  heart and, 138–139
  personal programs of, 138–143
  remedial, 137–138
  stress and, 131–143

Farrow, Mia, 183
Fitzgerald, F. Scott, 201, 206
  Tender is the Night, 200
Flu, *see* Influenza
Food
  survival and, 7–8
  see also Diet, Dieting
Forrestal, James V., 5
Franklin, Benjamin, 159
Free association technique, 160
French, John R. P., 52n
Freud, Sigmund, 15, 120–121, 123, 126, 196n
  on aggression, 103
  on the ego, 101–102
  Freudian theory, 158–161
Friedman, Dr. Meyer
  heart disease studies, 25–34
  Type A: Behavior and Your Heart (with Rosenman), 28n
Fromm, Erich, 215–216
  The Sane Society, 215n

Games for exercise, 137
Gastrectomy, 54
General Adaptation Syndrome, 18
Geriatric Institute (Bucharest), 198

Gerontology Research Center (Baltimore), 189
Giving, essence of, 10
Glands, *see* Adrenal gland; Pancreas; Pituitary gland; Thyroid gland
Glass, David C. (ed.)
  Neurophysiology and Emotion, 144
Glaucoma
  open angle glaucoma, 138
Glueck, Dr. Bernard, 192–193
Goldwag, Dr. William J., 179
Grace, Dr. William J.
  The Human Colon (with Wolf and Wolff), 60, 61n
Green Bay Packers, 92n
Groen, Dr. J. J.
  asthma studies, 71
Guillotin, Dr. J. I., 159
Gurdjieff, G. I., 185

Habit, stress and, 212–213
Hannibal, 131
Hare Krishna, 186
Harper's Bazaar, 148
Hartford, Conn., 192
Headache
  migraine, 5, 6, 32, 43–45, 120, 189–190
  tension headache, 43–44, 86, 89, 190
Heart
  biological feedback and, 189
  counting the heartbeat, 136
  exercise and, 138–139
  exertion and, 136–137
  see also Heart disease; *names of diseases*
Heart disease, 163, 177–178
  cardiovascular stress exercises, 134–136

emotional problems and, 34–37
in history, 23–25
predictive study of coronary disease, 224–235
stress and, 24–34
see also Cholesterol studies; Heart; names of diseases

Helpless-hopeless type, 104, 220

Heroin, 171

Hinkle, Lawrence, E., 73

Hippocrates, 23

Holmes, Thomas J., 12

Hormones
stress and, 108–109
see also Neuro-endocrine system; Thyrotrophic hormone

Horney, Karen, 120, 160, 161

Hostility, 120, 122
dependency and, 104–105, 160–161

Howells, John G.
Modern Perspectives in World Psychiatry, 117n

Humplik, Dr. Heinz, 148

Hypertension, 5, 23, 34, 37–42, 119, 163

Hyperthyroidism, 163

Hypnosis, 159–160, 193–196

Hypothalamus, 107, 108, 109–110

Hysteria, 159–160

Ichazo, Oscar, 187

Id, 102

Identity, see Self-identity

Immunity screen,
see Immunology: immunological system, stress and the immunity screen

Immunology, 62–82
allergies and, 70–73
auto-immunity, 74–75
immunological system, 63
cancer and, 75–82
infections and, 64–69
science of, 63–64
specific immunity, 66–69
stress and the immunity screen, 69

Industrialism, 9–12

Infant mortality rates, 6

Inflammation, 66, 73
corticoids and, 108

Influenza, 68

Injection therapy (Aslan), 198

Insomnia, 190

Institute of Living (Hartford), 192

Isometrics, 135

Isotonics, 140–141

Itch, 5

Jefferson, Thomas, 43

Jogging, 138, 139

Kasl, Stanislav V., 52n

Kennedy, John F., 133–134

Keyes, Ancel, 23–24

Kiefer, Durand, 192

Kierkegaard, Sørcn, 80, 161

King's Mirror, The, 200

Koch, Robert, 3, 63

Kramer, Jerry
Farewell to Football, 92n

Kraus, Dr. Hans, 84

La Jolla, Calif., 181

Laing, R. D.
The Divided Self, 116n

Lavoisier, Antoine, 159

Le Shan, Dr. Lawrence, 201, 220

"An Emotional Life History Pattern Associated with Neoplastic Disease," 81n
cancer studies, 79–82
Lewis, Sinclair, 31
Lie detector test, 116
Life magazine, 175, 176
Lindsay, John V., 203, 204–206
Lipoproteins, 156n
Los Angeles, Calif., 187
Logic, vs. emotions, 99–101
London School of Hygiene and Tropical Medicine, 136
Longevity, 6
Louis XVI (France), 159
Lourdes, France, 177
LSD, 171
Lymphatic system, 66

Machine age, human body and, 12
Mahesh Yogi, Maharishi, 183–184
Malignancy, *see* Cancer
Marijuana, 171, 185
Masters two-step test, 136
Maule, Tex, 139, 142
Running Scared, 139n
Mayo diet, 147
Mead Johnson & Co., 147
Measles, 68, 70
Medicine, taking of, 218–219
Medicine man (Indian), 194–195
Meditation
biological feedback and, 192–193
stress and, 182–187
Meekness, stress and, 214
Menninger, Karl, 95
Menninger, Dr. William, 177
Menninger Foundation, 190
Mesmer, F. A., 159

Mesomorphs, 146
Metastasis, 79
Methedrine ("speed"), 171
Metrecal, 147
Miami, Fla., 187
Migraine, *see* Headache
Miller, Dr. Neal E., 188–189
Mind
emotions vs. logic, 99–101
psychology of, 101–105
stress and, 99–105
Mobility, social
stress and, 9–10
Montana, Joe, 93
Montreal, Canada, 16
Moos, Dr. R. H.
rheumatoid studies, 88
Moreno, Dr. J. L., 180
Mozart, Wolfgang A., 10
Mumps, 68
Münchener Medizinische Wöchenschrift, 148
Murder, 95
Muscles, *see* Skeletal-muscular system
Mutation, 75–77

NASA, *see* National Aeronautics and Space Administration
National Aeronautics and Space Administration (NASA), 134
National Institute of Child Health and Human Development, 189
National Institute of Mental Health, 194
National Training Laboratories (NTL), 180
Navajo Indians, 194–195
Neuro-endocrine system
adrenal glands, 108, 112–114

cerebral cortex, 107–108, 109
endocrine hormones, 108
hypothalamus, 107, 108, 109–110
negative feedback, 108–109
pancreas, 113, 114, 115
pituitary gland, 110
stress and, 106–115
thyroid gland, 111
Neurosis, 160–161, 180
stress and, 42–43
New York, N.Y., 14, 177, 187, 203
New York State Addiction Control System, 170
Niehans, Dr. Paul, 198
Nor-adrenalin hormone, 112
Norstebo, Guttorm, 52n
NTL, *see* National Training Laboratories

Obesity, 153
medical research on, 154–156
stress and, 143–145
see also weight
Osler, Sir William, 3, 25

Palo Alto, Calif., 14
Pancreas, stress and, 113, 114, 115
Paris, France, 159
Pasteur, Louis, 3, 15, 19, 63
Penicillin, 64
Pentecostalism, 186
Pep pills, 171
Pharmacology, *see* Drugs
Pittsburgh, Pa., 187
Pituitary gland, 110
Placebos, 176–179
Pratt, Dr. J. H., 180
President's Council on Physical Fitness, 134, 140
Prison life, 13n

Proust, Marcel, *Remembrance of Things Past*, 32
Psychiatry
analytical, 158
for coronary patients, 37
hypertensives and, 40
see also Psychoanalysis; Psychotherapy
Psychoanalysis
cost factor, 196
Psychodrama, 180
Psychology, science of, 101–105, 158
Psychosomatics, 15, 164
stress and, 116–126
Psychotherapy, 128, 158–169
Freudian theory, 158–161
techniques of, 161–162
Psychotics, 121–123

Quakers (Society of Friends), 194
Quimby, Phineas, 159

Reich, Wilhelm, 160
Religion, stress and, 8–9, 128, 194
Repetition compulsion, 123
Respiratory problems
chronic diseases, 118
exercise and, 138
Responsibility, stress and, 207
Rheumatic fever, 34, 74
Richards, Dr. Victor
Cancer, the Wayward Cell, 77
Rogers, Carl, 181–182
Carl Rogers on Encounter Groups, 182n
Roman Catholicism, 194
Rosenfeld, Albert, 175
Rosenman, Dr. Ray
heart disease studies, 24–34

Rosenman, Dr. Ray *(cont.)*
Type A Behavior and Your Heart (with Friedman), 28n
Routine (loss of challenge), stress and, 13
Running, 137
Russell, Lillian, 145

San Diego, Calif., 187
San Francisco, Calif., 24, 27, 187
Sauna, 198
Sausalito, Calif., 32
Schachter, Dr. Stanley, 144–145
Second-chance syndrome, 221–222
Sedatives, 170–171, 172
Self-awareness, 186–187, 194
Self-identity, 208–216, 222–223
Self-punishment, 95
Selye, Hans, 63, 106, 108
stress studies, 15–19
Sensitivity groups, 179
Sexuality, 36, 61, 103, 110n, 120–121
Freudian theory, 160
stress and, 114
Sheldon, Dr. William, 146
Shock treatment, 197–199
Silverman, Dr. Samuel, 122, 166–169
Psychological Aspects of Physical Symptoms, 169n
Skeletal-muscular system, 83–96
accidents and, 90–96
arthritis, 86–89
backache and, 84–86
chronic muscle spasm, 85–86
muscular deficiency, 84–85
muscular tension, 121

tension headache and, 86
Sleep treatment, 197–198
Society
self-identity and, 208
taking and giving in, 9–12
Solomon, Dr. George F., 79
rheumatoid studies, 88–89
"Speed" *see* Methedrine
Spiegel, Dr. Herbert, 193–194, 195n
Sports Illustrated, 139
Stare, Frederick J., 148
Stimson, Dr. Barbara, 84
Stoyva, Dr. Johann, 190
Strep infections, 68
Stress
anger and, 214–215
death and, 123–124
disease and, 4–7
drive for success and, 200–216
early research on, 15–19
habit and, 212–213
meekness and, 214
patient-initiated cures, 195
personal responses to, 127–129
primal stresses, 7–12
responses to, 17–18, 116–126
responsibility and, 207
selecting among available treatments for, 195–199
Selye's studies on, 15–19
in space flight program, 207
see also Exercise; *names of diseases*
Success, drive for, 200–216
money and, 202–203
power and, 206–207
recognition and, 203–206
Suicide, 39n, 95, 215–216
Superego, 102
Support groups, 129, 179–182

Surgery, 219–220
Swimming, 137

T (Training) groups, 180
Tassajara, Japan, 192
Thyroid gland, 111
Thyrotrophic hormone, 110–111
TM, *see* Transcendental Meditation
Toilet training, bowel disorders and, 55
Tom (Dr. S. Wolf's associate), 48–51, 54
Toothache, 86
Tranquilizers, 170–171, 172
Transactional analysis, 160
Transcendental Meditation (TM), 182–185, 187, 192–193
Truman, Harry S, 5
Tuberculosis, 70n
group psychotherapy, 180
Tumor, *see* Cancer
Tuscaloosa, Ala., 14
Twiggy, 145
Typhus, 3

Ulcers, 5, 6–7, 39n, 50–55, 119, 162, 164–166, 177
Unconscious
Freudian concept of, 158–159

Vagotomy, 54
Van Gogh, Vincent, 206
Vegetables, home grown, 156–157
Vienna, Austria, 120, 148, 159
Virus, 76–77

Walking, 137
Wallace, Robert Keith, 184
War
health during wartime, 122

stress effects of, 38–39
Weber, Dr. Sonja, 84
Weight
endocrine malfunction, 147
ideal, 145–146
natural variations in physique, 146
overeating and, 143–145
testing for overweight, 148n
see also Diet, Dieting; Obesity
Weight Watchers, 153
Weill, Dr. Andrew, 186–187
Weiss, Dr. Edward
Psychosomatic Medicine (with English), 52, 57–59
Weiss, Dr. Theodore, 189
White, Dr. Paul Dudley, 23, 32
Wittkower, Eric D., 116–117
Wodehouse, P. G., 143
Wolf, Dr. Stewart, 36n, 119
digestive system/emotional stress studies, 48–51
Headaches: Their Nature and Treatment (with Wolff), 73n
The Human Colon (with Grace and Wolff), 60, 61n
The Stomach, 49n, 52
Wolff, Dr. Harold D., 13n, 49, 104, 122, 123
Headaches: Their nature and Treatment (with Wolf), 73n
The Human Colon (with Grace and Wolf), 60, 61n
hypertension studies, 38
migraine-personality studies, 44
Stress and Disease, 13n
Wolpe, Dr. Joseph, 162
World War II, 41, 50, 72, 84, 180

World War II *(cont.)*
  battle of Stalingrad, 38–39
Yoga, 128, 185, 192

Zen, 192
  Zen Buddhist Macrobiotic diet, 148
Zimbardo, F. G., 14

There's an epidemic with 27 million victims. And no visible symptoms.

It's an epidemic of people who can't read.

Believe it or not, 27 million Americans are functionally illiterate, about one adult in five.

The solution to this problem is you... when you join the fight against illiteracy. So call the Coalition for Literacy at toll-free 1-800-228-8813 and volunteer.

Volunteer Against Illiteracy. The only degree you need is a degree of caring.